Tales from the Vienna Woods
and other Plays

Studies in Austrian Literature, Culture, and Thought

Translation Series

Ödön von Horváth

Tales from the Vienna Woods and other Plays

Translated and with an
Afterword by Michael Mitchell

ARIADNE PRESS
Riverside, California

Translated from the German
© Thomas Sessler Verlag, Wien

Library of Congress Cataloging-in-Publication Data

Horváth, Ödön von, 1901-1938
  [Plays. English. Selections]
  Tales from the Vienna Woods and other plays / Ödön von Horváth ; translated and with an afterword by Michael Mitchell.
      p. cm. -- (Studies in Austrian literature, culture and thought. Translation series)
  Contents: The Italian evening — Tales from the Vienna Woods — Casimir and Caroline — Faith, love, hope.
  ISBN 1-57241-108-2
  I. Mitchell, Michael, 1941- II. Title. III. Series.

PT2617.O865 A 6 2002
832'.912--dc21
                                            2002071746

Cover Design:
Art Director, Designer: George McGinnis

Copyright ©2002
by Ariadne Press
270 Goins Court
Riverside, CA 92507

All rights reserved.
No part of this publication may be reproduced or transmitted
in any form or by any means without formal permission.
Printed in the United States of America.
ISBN 1-57241-108-2
(paperback original)

Ödön von Horváth

With the kind permission of the Thomas Sessler Verlag, Vienna

CONTENTS

The Italian Evening 1

Tales from the Vienna Woods 55

Casimir and Caroline 131

Faith, Love, Hope 191

Afterword 239

The Italian Evening

Play in Seven Scenes

2 *The Italian Evening*

CHARACTERS

CITY COUNCILMAN AMMETSBERGER
KRANZ
ENGELBERT
BETZ
INNKEEPER
KARL
MARTIN
MARTIN'S COMRADES
COMRADE FROM MAGDEBURG
FASCIST
LIEUTENANT
MAJOR
CZERNOWITZ
ADELE
ANNA
LENI
FRAU DVORAK
TWO WHORES
FRAU HINTERBERGER
THE LEIMSIEDLER SISTERS
REPUBLICANS AND FASCISTS

Location: Small town in southern Germany

Time: 1930-?

SCENE ONE

In Josef Lehninger's inn. Kranz, Engelbert and Councilman Ammetsberger are playing cards. Karl is kibitzing, Betz contentedly sipping his beer, Martin reading the paper, the innkeeper picking his nose. It is Sunday morning and the sun is shining. Silence.

BETZ Anything new in the big wide world, Martin?
MARTIN No, nothing at all. The workers paying the taxes and the employers screwing the state left, right and center is hardly something new. Or don't you agree?
BETZ (*empties his glass*)
MARTIN And the gentlemen who receive a pension from the Republic organizing a reactionary imperial parade with a field mass and small-bore rifle competition, and we Republicans unable to do a thing about it, that's nothing new either. Or don't you agree?
BETZ It's a democratic republic we're living in, Martin, old pal.
(*Outside, a fascist unit with a military band marches past. All, apart from Councilman Ammetsberger and the Innkeeper, go over to the window and watch the procession in silence. Only when it's passed do they come back to life.*)
COUNCILMAN AMMETSBERGER (*cards in his hand*) Talk of an acute threat to our democratic republic is nonsense, naturally. For one thing, the forces of reaction lack any ideological foundation.
ENGELBERT Well said!
COUNCILMAN AMMETSBERGER Comrades! As long as we have our Republican Defense Association and as long as I have the honor to be chairman of our local section, the Republic can sleep in peace.
MARTIN Good night, then!
KRANZ Permission to speak, Mr. Chairman. I have a proposal. I would like to suggest from now on we continue with our cards and ignore these Teutonic court jesters and their so-called German Day.
ENGELBERT And their Third Reich!

COUNCILMAN AMMETSBERGER Carried nem. con. (*shuffles and deals*)
KARL And what's going to happen this evening?
COUNCILMAN AMMETSBERGER What about this evening?
KARL Regarding our Italian Evening this evening —
COUNCILMAN AMMETSBERGER (*interrupts*) Our Italian Evening is going ahead this evening. Of course it is. Or is there anyone who thinks the Republican Defense Association is going to let some reactionary or other stop them putting on an Italian Evening here, in the establishment of our old friend, Josef Lehninger, whenever *we* want? Our Republican Italian Evening is going ahead this evening, despite Mussolini and his henchmen. Ace of diamonds. (*plays*)
ENGELBERT You didn't know that?!
KARL How should I have known?
BETZ I made an official announcement.
ENGELBERT But Comrade Karl wasn't there. As usual. Clubs.
KARL But I can't be around all the time.
ENGELBERT He even missed the last parade. All this womanizing.
KRANZ Solo.
COUNCILMAN AMMETSBERGER Misère.
ENGELBERT From the hand?
COUNCILMAN AMMETSBERGER From the hand — and I'll win hands down.
KARL (*to Betz*) Do I have to put up with this? All this talk of womanizing?
BETZ You have to admit that women do get in the way of your duty to the Republic —
KARL But those are personal, intimate concerns, if you don't mind. If you *don't* mind.
(*Outside another fascist unit with a military band marches past. They all listen, but no one goes to the window.*
Silence.)
BETZ Yes, well, everything's relative, isn't it?

MARTIN Relative?! It's a damn disgrace, that's what it is! While the forces of reaction are arming themselves, we good little Republicans organize Italian Evenings!
BETZ It's incredible, isn't it, how strong the forces of reaction are getting.
MARTIN Incredible my ass! You can work it out for yourself. Those who have the economic power have right on their side. It's a well-known fact, that, only you on the committee don't seem to know it. I keep telling myself you do want to know, but sometimes it's pretty difficult —
ENGELBERT Oh, come on!
BETZ Your trouble is, you're a pessimist.
MARTIN Like shit I am.
COUNCILMAN AMMETSBERGER And always picking quarrels. Just for the sake of it.
(*Silence*)
MARTIN (*slowly getting up*) Tell me, Councilman Ammetsberger, do you know a certain Karl Marx.
COUNCILMAN AMMETSBERGER (*thumping the table*) Do I know my Marx!? Of course I know my Marx! And I'm not going to put up with such insinuations!
ENGELBERT Quite right!
KRANZ Solo!
COUNCILMAN AMMETSBERGER Or do you think, you starry-eyed idealist, do you think that — to put it in a nutshell — when Marxism comes there'll be — to put it in a nutshell — paradise on earth?
MARTIN What your nutshell's got to do with it, I don't know. And what you understand by paradise I don't know either, but I can well imagine what you understand by Marxism. That understood? I know what *I* understand by it, and I believe in it!
KRANZ Solo, for God's sake! (*plays a card*)
(*Silence*)
BETZ D'you know what I can't do any more?
MARTIN No.
BETZ Believe.

(*Silence*)
MARTIN I can well believe you can't believe in it. You can't believe because you don't have to. You're not a proletarian, you office clerk, you.
BETZ *Senior* office clerk, as it happens, but naturally that's neither here nor there.
MARTIN Naturally.
BETZ Naturally's got nothing to do with it!
MARTIN (*gives im a baffled look*) Oh, you can go kiss my arse! (*dashes off carrying his newspaper*)
COUNCILMAN AMMETSBERGER Such elegance of expression — (*Silence*)
INNKEEPER D'you think it's going to rain? Every time I slaughter a pig the weather goes and ruins my Italian Evening.
BETZ I don't think it will.
INNKEEPER Why? Because it's your Italian Evening?
BETZ No. Because the depression over Ireland has given way to high pressure over the Bay of Biscay.
COUNCILMAN AMMETSBERGER Quite right.
INNKEEPER And who says so?
BETZ The official state meteorological station.
INNKEEPER You know what you can do with your officials!
MARTIN (*returns, goes over to Betz and places a leaflet on the table in front of him*) There!
BETZ What am I meant to do with that?
MARTIN Read it!
BETZ Why should I read that stupid fascist stuff?
MARTIN Because it might well interest you?
BETZ Not in the slightest.
MARTIN (*raising his voice*) In fact, it might well interest all you gentlemen here.
THE GENTLEMEN (*look up*)
COUNCILMAN AMMETSBERGER What's he on about now? He's always got some ax to grind.

BETZ (*starts skimming through the leaflet mechanically, then suddenly stops and thumps the table with his fist*) What!? That's outrageous! Outrageous, isn't it Josef?
INNKEEPER (*uneasy, tries to slip away*)
BETZ (*fixes his eyes on him, an outraged look on his face*) Stop! Stop! Josef, my friend, this should interest you more than anyone. Do you know what it says?
INNKEEPER (*embarrassed*) No . . .
BETZ Oh, so you can't read?
INNKEEPER (*with a despairing smile*) No . . .
BETZ Illiterate, are we?
COUNCILMAN AMMETSBERGER (*has been listening*) What's all this about, then?
INNKEEPER Nothing, guys, nothing —
BETZ Nothing? You don't say, my dear Josef? I think you're a top-class bastard, Josef.
INNKEEPER You shouldn't say things like that, Heinrich.
BETZ I'll say it again, my dear Josef.
COUNCILMAN AMMETSBERGER What for?
KRANZ For God's sake —
MARTIN (*interrupting*) Just a moment!
BETZ Yes, just a moment. This here is what's called an order of the day. Our fascist friends' order of the day for today, their so-called German Day. (*hands the leaflet to Karl*) Josef, we Republicans are your regulars, and you've gone and sold your soul. Just for money!
KARL The cheek of it! Listen to this, comrades: (*reads*) "4 pm — 6 pm: band in garden of Josef Lehninger's inn."
KRANZ What band?
KARL The fascist band! Shame on you!
BETZ It's a disgrace, that's what it is! Josef — our dear comrade Josef — reserving our table for the reactionaries!
KARL And the Republicans, he imagines, will wait their turn, like good little boys, and buy all his stuff for their Italian Evening!
MARTIN The scraps our friends the fascists have left!
ENGELBERT Hear, hear!

INNKEEPER Look, you've got hold of the wrong end of the stick —
MARTIN Oh yes? Pull the other one!
KARL That's unscrupulous, that is!
INNKEEPER I'm not unscrupulous, guys. It's not me, it's my wife.
BETZ Stuff and nonsense!
INNKEEPER It's not stuff and nonsense at all. You guys don't know my wife. She doesn't give a shit for the political situation. She doesn't give a fucking damn who eats her fucking sausages. And here was me, ass that I was, dreaming of a nice quiet life in my old days! And if I don't put out the old black-white-and-red flag, that's sixty helpings of roast pork down the spout. I always said it was a stupid idea to change the flag after the War. God, I don't know whether I'm coming or going.
KRANZ If you weren't a friend, I'd spit in your face, Josef.
ENGELBERT That's right. You tell him!
(*Silence*)
INNKEEPER (*in desperation*) Christ Almighty! I'm going to get pissed. Then I'll shoot my old woman and jump out of the window. But first I'll set fire to the whole damn place. (*exit*)
COUNCILMAN AMMETSBERGER Oh, for heaven's sake! Every time I get a decent hand all hell breaks loose. (*raises his voice*) But I'd like to see the power that has the power to stop us holding our Italian Evening this evening. Comrades, we will not budge an inch, even if the forces of reaction from the whole world were united against us! Our Republican Italian Evening is going ahead this evening, as announced. Even the good Herr Josef Lehninger won't thwart our plans! Keep a note of the cards you had and we'll continue our game on my veranda. Come on, comrades.
MARTIN Three cheers for our brave councilman Ammetsberger!
KRANZ Cynic!
ALL (*leave the inn*)

SCENE TWO

Street. All the houses have black-white-and-red flags out, because the local branch of the fascists is organizing a "German Day," as is announced on a banner. A section is just marching past, with flags, band and small-bore rifles, followed by some of the right-wing German nationalists among the community. Frau Dvorak and Leni are among them.

LENI I've had about enough now, I'm stopping here.
FRAU DVORAK That's a pity, young lady.
LENI The music's okay, but I don't really go for these men in their uniforms. They all look the same, it's so boring. And they tend to be so conceited, so cocky. There's something in me that just can't stand it.
FRAU DVORAK I can well believe that. It's because you can't remember the way we were before the war.
LENI I have to go off left here.
FRAU DVORAK Fräulein Leni, you could do me a big favor —
LENI Of course.
FRAU DVORAK Your major must have some very splendid uniforms —
LENI Yes, he does. Because earlier on he spent some time in the colonies they stole from us after the war.
FRAU DVORAK Do you think you could ask the major whether he wouldn't mind selling me one of those old uniforms? You've nothing to lose.
LENI What do you mean by that?
FRAU DVORAK Just a manner of speaking.
(*Silence*)
LENI What would you do with the uniform?
FRAU DVORAK (*smiling*) Look at it.
LENI Just look at it, that's all?
FRAU DVORAK It all depends how you look at it —
LENI No, I'm sorry, I find that a bit weird, I think —

FRAU DVORAK (*suddenly furious*) You stupid girl! You young people have no ideals any more! (*dashes off; a drum roll*)
KARL (*enters and recognizes Leni*) Now isn't that a coincidence?!
LENI Well I never! Karl!
KARL It certainly is.
LENI How do you mean?
KARL Us meeting like this, just by coincidence.
LENI Get away, it happens all the time.
KARL It certainly does.
(*Silence*)
LENI I haven't much time just now, Karl.
KARL Me neither. But I've a suggestion to make, Leni.
LENI What kind of suggestion?
KARL Why don't two beautiful people like us meet this evening, that's what I'd like to suggest. I was going to suggest it yesterday, but the opportunity never arose —
LENI You don't have to lie to me, Karl.
(*Silence*)
KARL (*with a brusque bow*) Fräulein Leni, I've never had to lie to a woman in all my life. I'm a decent honest guy, I'll have you know.
LENI I didn't mean to insult you —
KARL You couldn't insult me.
LENI (*staring at him*) What do you mean by that?
KARL I mean that you can't insult me because I like you — at most you could hurt me. That's what I meant by it. Sorry.
(*Silence*)
LENI I think you're bad news.
KARL Bad? There's no such thing as bad people, Fräulein, only very poor people. Sorry.
(*Silence*)
LENI Okay, but I'm only going to wait ten minutes at most —
KARL Me five.
LENI (*with a smile*) Then if you don't mind, Mr. Bad News — (*exit*)
MARTIN AND BETZ (*enter*)

The Italian Evening 11

MARTIN (*turns to watch Leni as she hurries past him, then gives Karl a mocking look*)
KARL By the way, Martin, I assume that not only registered members and associate members are welcome at our Italian Evening this evening but sympathizers as well —
MARTIN If you want.
KARL I've just invited someone, you see. A young lady I know who's sympathetic to our cause.
MARTIN The one who just left?
KARL D'you know her?
MARTIN Unfortunately.
KARL Why unfortunately?
MARTIN Because she's a pigheaded young woman.
KARL Seems to me she's got a certain something —
MARTIN Of course she's got a certain something, but it's not her certain something we're talking about. What I'm saying is she's a pigheaded young woman as far as politics is concerned. She's a born reactionary, for God's sake! How anyone can go round with something like that!
KARL You don't understand, Martin. We're both committed Republicans, yes, but there is a difference. You're a worker and I'm a musician. You're at the assembly line while I'm playing Mozart and Kalman in a palm court somewhere. I'm an artist, you see, and that's why I'm more of an individualist. My personal interests seem to be stronger, but that's an illusion, actually, because with me everything goes into my art.
MARTIN (*grinning*) That's a neat excuse —
KARL So I owe it to myself not to restrict myself politically as far as my sex life's concerned. Excuse me. (*exit*)
MARTIN Tally ho!
(*Silence*)
BETZ Martin, you know I respect you, even though you can sometimes be unpleasantly scathing. But I think your way of assessing the world political situation overlooks something very important, namely our natural love life. Recently I've been looking at Professor Freud's works, you know. You mustn't forget that our

ego is surrounded by aggressive urges which are eternally at war with our libido, and which can come out as suicidal urges, or as sadism, masochism, rape, murder —
MARTIN Keep your perversions to yourself, you filthy swine.
BETZ But they're your perversions, too.
MARTIN Oh, yes??
BETZ Or have you never given Anna a little pinch or whatever when you — you know, just at that moment —
MARTIN That's no fucking business of yours.
BETZ But they're not perversions at all, they're just basic drives. And our aggressive urges play an overriding role in realizing socialism, I'll have you know. They act as an inhibitory mechanism. I'm afraid you're just burying your head in the sand in this respect.
MARTIN You know what you can do with your aggressive urges? (*turns on his heel and leaves*)

SCENE THREE

In the town park. Lots of flags, the air filled with military music. Two whores are standing at the corner. It is already late afternoon. Councilman Ammetsberger walks past. The women wink.

FIRST (*old and skinny*) D'you know him?
SECOND (*young and fat*) He's okay.
FIRST I think he's something to do with the town. Some big shot.
SECOND Probably.
(*the flags flutter in the breeze*)
SECOND (*looks up*) If only there weren't those flags —
FIRST But flags are really uplifting.
SECOND No — when I see flags like that I feel as if the war was still on.
FIRST (*using her lipstick*) I'm not saying anything against the World War. That would be ungrateful.
(*silence*)
SECOND (*still looking up*) Flapping like that — what's the use for the likes of us?
FIRST I find agricultural exhibitions are the best, or any kind of artistic event. Patriotic ceremonies like this aren't bad either.
FASCIST (*walks past*)
FIRST (*goes over to him*)
FASCIST Dismiss!
(*pause*)
SECOND Actually it's the war that's to blame.
FIRST What for?
SECOND Me.
FIRST Stuff and nonsense! They all use the war as an excuse.
ANNA (*enters and sits down on a bench with her back to the two whores; she's waiting*)
FIRST Who's that?
SECOND I don't know her.
FIRST She looks so new. And yet she looks like someone —
SECOND (*with a grin*) Like you.

FIRST (*stares at her*) That was a mean thing to say, Agnes.
THREE FASCISTS (*walk past Anna*)
ANNA (*avoids their looks*)
THE FASCISTS (*stop in front of her and grin at her*)
ANNA (*stands up and makes to leave*)
MARTIN (*blocks her way, greets her with a nod and talks to her*)
THE FASCISTS AND THE WHORES (*listen but can't hear anything*)
ANNA And?
MARTIN No and. He's wriggled his way out of things once again, has our town councilman Ammetsberger. It's beneath his dignity as a Republican, he said, to abandon his Italian Evening because of that lot's German Day and Lehninger's double-dealing. Typical party hack of the worst sort. Everything's taking its inevitable course.
ANNA Corrupt.
MARTIN It's profits that rule. That means it's antisocial elements that run things. And they create a world after their own image. No question. They'll see that they dance to a different tune at their Italian Evening tonight.
THE FASCISTS (*start chatting up the whores*)
ANNA Do you know what the comrades are saying?
MARTIN What?
ANNA That you have a future.
MARTIN (*shrugs his shoulders*) Well, they know me, don't they? But I'd have to leave. Go to some big city.
ANNA And I have the feeling they're just waiting for you.
MARTIN There's not enough scope for me here. Someone else could do what I'm doing here just as well.
ANNA No, there's no one else could do it the way you do.
MARTIN You know I don't like to hear you say that.
ANNA But it's true. If everyone was like you we'd all be the better for it.
MARTIN But I can't help it. It's just the way I am. That I'm more intelligent, that I have more energy — that just obliges me to work with even greater commitment for what's right. I'm fed up with

The Italian Evening 15

hearing I'm an exception. For Christ's sake! (*bawls at her*) I'm not, and just you remember that!

ANNA There are other ways of telling someone you're not an exception —

(*silence*)

MARTIN Anna, time's whizzing by and there are more burning questions than the way you put something. Don't forget you have obligations.

ANNA Me?

MARTIN Obligations demand commitment.

ANNA Martin, you're talking as if I were neglecting my duty —

MARTIN What makes you say that? That would be arrogance. Don't make something simple more complicated than need be. I just wanted to remind you of what we discussed yesterday. Just do it, eh? (*exit*)

TWO FASCISTS (*have gone off with the whores*)

THIRD FASCIST (*stares at Anna*)

ANNA (*abruptly*) Well?

THIRD FASCIST (*grins*)

ANNA (*smiling*) Well?

KARL (*appears behind the fascist*)

ANNA (*starts*)

KARL Excuse me.

THIRD FASCIST (*grins, gives Anna a mockingly elegant bow and leaves*)

(*silence*)

KARL (*with suppressed agitation*)Do excuse me, madam.

ANNA Idiot!

KARL For God's sake, Anna! You with that fascist — the world doesn't make sense any more. Who is it who's mad, me or you?

ANNA You! Here I am, trying to set something up and you come crashing in without thinking, like a bull in a china shop!

KARL Without thinking?

ANNA And without Party discipline.

KARL Without Party discipline?! Martin's just been bawling me out for taking up with a woman with no interest in politics and

here's his Anna flirting with a fascist! Christ, I think I must be going off my head. Ripe for the loonybin!
ANNA Just calm down now.
KARL Poor old Martin!
ANNA But I'm not doing anything Martin doesn't know about.
KARL (*staring at her*) Sorry?
ANNA I'm not doing anything wrong.
KARL Oh no?
ANNA It's all OK. Martin just wants to get a bit more detailed information about their small-bore rifles, so I've to chat one of the fascists up a bit, pump him —
KARL (*lights a cigarette*)
ANNA And what did you think?
KARL Me? Sorry.
ANNA That was very insulting —
KARL I'm sorry.
ANNA You should be ashamed of yourself.
(*silence*)
KARL Anna, I've had all sorts of experiences as far as sex is concerned and it's easy to get cynical after a while. Especially if you're an observant type. Of course, you're a paragon of morality. You've changed quite a lot.
ANNA (*with a smile*) Thanks.
KARL Not at all. You used to be different, you know. In the old days.
ANNA (*nods*) Yes, in the old days.
KARL You weren't so strict then.
(*silence*)
ANNA (*suddenly serious*) So?
KARL When I look at you now I can feel an attack of morality coming on. Martin's right, I shouldn't take things so casually. Here I am, out for a date again. She's not interested in politics, but — (*looks at his wristwatch*)
ANNA In your place I'd try to be a good influence on her.
KARL God, you're so right. I will. Honest.
ANNA How often have you said that before?

KARL Anna, it's more important to see where you've gone wrong than to avoid doing anything wrong. If I give you my word of honor that at our Italian Evening this evening I'll exercise passive resistance, so to speak —
ANNA What do you mean by that?
KARL Well, for example I won't dance at all. Not a single step. Not even with myself. There's no point in going through life as if you're just an animal, only thinking of satisfying your lower instincts — (*automatically puts his arm round her waist, without realizing what he is going*)
ANNA (*slowly removes his hand and gives him a long look*)
KARL (*becomes aware of what he has done. Silence.*)
KARL (*insidiously*) I still think it's funny, what Martin's doing —
ANNA What?
KARL I couldn't do that.
ANNA What?!
KARL I just can't imagine what his feelings for you are. I mean, are they normal, or what?
ANNA What are you getting at?
KARL I'm just interested. I mean, asking something like that of you, sending you out on the game — politically, of course, politically. D'you think he had to force himself?
ANNA Force himself?
KARL Yes.
(*silence*)
ANNA Of course not! You're just trying to confuse me, but you won't succeed. I know Martin better. He's way above the lot of us. I was stupid, idiotic, dishonest, petty, ugly, and he dragged me up out of it. I was never happy with myself. Now I am.
KARL (*sketches a bow*)
ANNA Now my life has some meaning, you know? (*goes off slowly*)
KARL Excuse me! (*looks at his watch, walks up and down, waiting*)

LENI (*enters*) Hi there, Karl. I'm just glad you're still here. I'm sorry but I couldn't get away earlier.
KARL We've plenty of time still. Anyway, there's nothing wrong with arriving a bit late.
LENI Why so sad, then?
KARL Sad?
LENI That tone! Like a voice from the grave! (*smiles*)
KARL I've just had an experience that's made me think. A political experience. We ought to me more aware of what's going on in the world. I think there must be a curse on me.
LENI Never, Karl! A man with a walk like that! (*laughs*)
KARL What's that?! (*gives her a stare*)
LENI (*falls silent*)
(*Pause*)
KARL Young woman, it seems you don't understand what I'm saying. It'd take me hours to explain it to you. The future looks black to me.
LENI Get away! A man like you, a man —
KARL It's the men who despair nowadays, especially me because I'm closer to political events. You're not interested in politics?
LENI No.
KARL But you should be.
LENI Why are you talking about them now, though?
KARL It's in your interest.
LENI You trying to provoke me?
KARL It's your duty as a citizen —
LENI Why're you trying to spoil everything for me. I was so looking forward to your Italian Evening.
(*silence*)
KARL I'm not the kind of man who plucks a flower just like that. I need some kind of contact, personal contact, and for me that means politics.
LENI Oh, pull the other one! I bet you don't even believe that yourself.
KARL But I do! For example, I could never have a long-term relationship with a woman who had a different way of thinking.
LENI You men all have the same way of thinking.

The Italian Evening   19

(*pause*)
KARL You're German, aren't you?
LENI Yes.
KARL You see, that's the trouble with us Germans. We don't bother with politics, we're not a political nation. There's masses of people here who have no idea who's running the country.
LENI I couldn't care less. It won't make any difference. I just make sure I get by, that's all.
KARL Seems to me you lack solidarity.
LENI Oh all these big words!
KARL Seems to me you don't even know who the President is?
LENI What do I care what these people are called.
KARL I bet you don't know who the Chancellor is?
LENI No, don't know him either.
KARL That's appalling! And typically German. Can you imagine a Frenchwoman who didn't know that?
LENI Why don't you go to France then?
(*pause*)
KARL Who's the minister of the interior? How many ministers are there? Roughly?
LENI If you don't shut up on the spot, I'm off.
KARL It's beyond belief!
(*pause*)
LENI This wasn't quite how I imagined this evening.
KARL Me neither.
LENI You go out — and then you're assaulted like that.
KARL (*looks at his watch*) It's about time.
LENI I don't think I want to go anymore.
KARL (*suddenly put his arms round her and kisses her*)
LENI (*doesn't resist*)
KARL (*looks her deep in the eyes and gives an anguished smile*) Oh yes, the minister of the interior — (*pulls her to him again*)

SCENE FOUR

In the town park by the monument to the former ruling prince. Two young men are painting his face red. A third is on look-out. It is already getting quite dark. In the distance the fascist band is playing the Bavarian Parade March — the "Bayrischer Defiliermarsch" — by Adolf Scherzer.

FIRST YOUNG MAN They'll get a big surprise tomorrow when they see how much His Majesty's changed. — His Majesty's gone red in the face — blood-red —
SECOND What a proud look he has.
FIRST (*slaps His Majesty's face with the brush*) Pity he's only got one face.
THIRD Watch out!
SECOND Hey?
THIRD My God, there's two of them coming.
SECOND Let's get the hell out of here.
FIRST Finished! (*quickly off with his comrades*)
(*Now it is almost completely dark*)
ANNA (*enters with a fascist*)
FASCIST It really is a beautiful town you've got here. It must make you feel particularly proud, Fräulein, coming from this town.
ANNA Yes, I am proud to come from this town.
FASCIST Honor thy native land! And what a convenient park you have here —
ANNA Shall we sit down?
FASCIST Allow me! (*they sit down*)
ANNA I'm a bit tired, you see. I've been following the march all day.
FASCIST Is military music in your blood too?
ANNA In my blood? You bet — (*lying*) My father was a sergeant in the army.
FASCIST Atten-tion!
(*silence*)
That larger-than-life-size statue over there, that's the monument to His Majesty, isn't it?

The Italian Evening

ANNA Yes.
FASCIST I've already had the honor of having it pointed out to me. We had an internal group discussion here this morning — it really is a handsome monument that, very stylish. Pity it's so dark already, you can't see it properly to admire it.
ANNA Was your internal group discussion a very solemn affair?
FASCIST Oh, very much so.
ANNA What were you discussing?
FASCIST Our mission. It's just not true what cowardly paid hacks say, that all life consists of is suffering, enjoying ourselves and dying. We have a mission to carry out down here! Some feel it more strongly, others hardly at all. In us it burns like a sacrificial flame! We will keep going to the bitter end.
(*silence*)
ANNA There's one thing I'd like to know.
FASCIST Ask away.
ANNA You see, I'm still pretty ignorant politically and I don't really know very much about your movement —
FASCIST (*interrupts her*) A woman's place is in the home. Her sole duty is to provide support for the warrior!
ANNA Yes, but there was one thing I wanted to ask about the future. Roughly —
FASCIST Ask no more, Fräulein, please. It is a sacred secret and my lips are sealed.
(*pause*)
It just doesn't make sense when people try to claim we're not a proletarian party. I know what I'm talking about. I'm an educated man and I'm not stupid, either. I'm a pharmacist.
ANNA It's getting dark now.
FASCIST (*dully*) Yes, dark.
(*pause*)
As dark as it is inside me. I can hardly see you any more, Fräulein — your blond hair —
ANNA But I'm not blond, I'm brunette.
FASCIST Dark blond, dark blond — Beware, blond maiden, beware! You know of whom! — It was the Jews who made us get involved in the War. In 1914 they could see the writing was on the

wall. The time could have arrived when the nations might have come to suspect the truth. Just imagine if the world had been struck by an epidemic, then people would have seen the Jews were to blame! — Blond maiden, I feel great joy within me that you have allowed me to speak with you like this —
ANNA I usually ignore men who speak to me in the street, but —
FASCIST But?
ANNA But people like you — No, don't! — No, please leave me alone, please!
FASCIST Very good, Fräulein. As you wish.
(pause)
ANNA I can't just — you know what.
FASCIST But we weren't just. We've been talking for quite a while, first of all about art, then about your beautiful city and now about the renewal our movement will bring.
(silence. Suddenly shouting at her) And do you know what's made the country go to the dogs? Materialism, that's what! And I'll tell you how it came about, I know all about that. My father's had his own shop for twenty-three years. That's the way things were. Now wherever you go the Jews have already bought everything up. They get everywhere with their cut-throat ways and drag everything down with them and that's the way materialism spread more and more. The trouble is, we've turned into a lot of women! It's high time we started wearing the trousers again and remembered we are Teutons! *(throws himself on her)*
ANNA No! Don't. *(resists)*
(Now the monument is lit up and His Majesty's red head can be seen.)
FASCIST *(letting go of Anna, in a hoarse voice)* What? — His Majesty violated — desecrated! Revenge! Germany awake!
(In the distance a Nazi song?)

SCENE FIVE

In the garden of Lehninger's inn. A band is playing.

FASCISTS (*drinking beer and singing "The Lorelei"*)
Whence comes this mysterious feeling
That fills my heart with dread?
A tale of a song so compelling
Goes round and round in my head.
The air is cool, night is falling,
And smoothly flows the Rhine —
FASCIST (*breaks in with "Die Wacht am Rhein"*) O Rhine, the Rhine, our German Rhine —
ALL FASCISTS To guard thy banks our oath we bind.
Dear Fatherland you're safe behind,
Dear Fatherland you're safe behind
Our watch along the Rhine, the German Rhine,
Our watch along the Rhine, the German Rhine!
FASCISTS (*brandishing their steins*) Heil! Heil! Heil! (*drink*)
(*The band plays "Stolz weht die Flagge schwarz-weiß-rot," the song of the old imperial German navy.*)
LIEUTENANT (*with a map; he beckons one of the fascists over*) Our night maneuvers: behind this marsh is, say, the French position, right next to the English artillery. Above and below are the Bolsheviks. You follow me?
FASCIST Sir!
LIEUTENANT And where are we? We're here. In the forest. The German forest. Symbolic even. And we're attacked. Of course. You can see if you look at history that we Germans have never done anything to harm another nation. For the sake of argument, let's assume the whole world is against us —
INNKEEPER Excuse me, Lieutenant.
LIEUTENANT Lehninger?
INNKEEPER Lieutenant, I need the garden, now —
LIEUTENANT What's all this about?
INNKEEPER It's getting time . . . You have to leave now —
LIEUTENANT You have the cheek to —

INNKEEPER No, Lieutenant, I have a duty — a patriotic duty. If you don't leave now you'll be late for all those night maneuvers *Pause.*
LIEUTENANT (*dismisses the fascist; calls out*) Czernowitz!
CZERNOWITZ (*a college student*) Yes, sir!
LIEUTENANT The major is waiting for us in the forest. The major will give his talk in the forest, in our German forest. You have finished it?
CZERNOWITZ Yes, sir! (*hands over a few pages out of a school notebook*)
LIEUTENANT Title?
CZERNOWITZ What the Japanese have the Germans to thank for?
LIEUTENANT That's right. — My God! Why didn't you write out a neat copy, man?
CZERNOWITZ You don't know my father, sir. All he cares about is my schoolwork. My family doesn't understand me, sir. Recently, when I said how pleased I was that we had so many enemies, it's a matter of honor for us, he thumped me one. If it wasn't for my mother, sir — my mother's then only one who understands me — my father's a liberal.
(*pause*)
LIEUTENANT Dismiss!
CZERNOWITZ (*does an about-face*)
LIEUTENANT Fall in!
FASCISTS (*fall in*)
LIEUTENANT Attention! Right about turn! Squad — by the right — quick march!
FASCISTS (*march off, the band playing the "Bayrischer Defiliermarsch"*)
INNKEEPER
(*lowers the black-white-and-red flag of the Empire and raises the black-red-and-gold flag of the Republic.*)

(*It is dark and the Republican Italian Evening is getting under way, with garlands and Chinese lanterns, a brass band and dancing. Members of the Party and sympathizers come into the inn garden to the strains of Fucik's "Entrance of the Gladiators," led*

The Italian Evening 25

by Councilman Ammetsberger, Kranz, Betz and Engelbert together with their wives. Karl and Leni are also among them. Martin comes as well, with his comrades and with a dark and determined look on his face; they sit well apart from the others.)

COUNCILMAN AMMETSBERGER Ladies and gentlemen! Comrades! Only a few hours ago it still looked as if a higher fate, in its hostility to mankind and not in the least to we Republicans, had determined that our dearest wish, our longed-for dream, our Italian Evening, was not to become reality. Comrades! Speaking in the name of the committee it is my happy position to be able to tell you that we have surmounted our fate. Looking round at all this festive splendor, at the rejoicing in all these expectant faces, both young and old, makes me appreciate just what we have surmounted! Let me just finish by saying it is my fervent wish that this open-air gala, our Republican Italian Evening will be an unforgettable experience for everyone present. Three cheers for the German people united in our Republic! Hip hip —
ALL APART FROM MARTIN'S COMRADES *(rise)* hooray!
COUNCILMAN AMMETSBERGER Hip hip —
ALL hooray!
COUNCILMAN AMMETSBERGER Hip hip —
ALL hooray!
(a flourish from the band)
COUNCILMAN AMMETSBERGER Please be seated.
ENGELBERT Ladies and gentlemen! Comrades! Sympathizers. I'm delighted we're all here. Please take your partners and line up for a quadrille.
(Councilman Ammetsberger, Betz, Kranz, Engelbert dance a quadrille with their ladies; Martin and his comrades look on with grim expressions on their faces. Then the band plays a waltz.)
ENGELBERT Ladies' choice! Ladies' choice!
MARTIN *(to his comrades)* No one's to dance. Discipline, remember, discipline! discipline and opposition!
SOME GIRLS *(want to dance with Martin's comrades but are turned away.)*
LENI *(to Karl)* May I have the pleasure now, then?

KARL (*remains silent*)
LENI For the last time, may I have the pleasure?
KARL (*remains silent*)
LENI How can you let a girl keep asking like that?
KARL Do you think it's easy for me?
LENI What's the point of coming here then if we're not going to dance?
KARL There's a deeper meaning to it.
LENI Call yourself a man? And you're too frightened to venture onto the dance floor.
KARL A man can break many things, but never his word of honor.
LENI A real man can do anything. No. Take your hand away.
KARL What hand?
LENI Your hand.
KARL You don't know what inner conflict is — otherwise you wouldn't appeal to my manhood like that — (*without really meaning to he finds he is dancing with her — anticlockwise round the floor*)
FIRST COMRADE Hey, Martin, didn't he give your Anna his word of honor he was our man?
MARTIN He pledged his word of honor to my Anna that he wouldn't dance a single step, that he'd make a stand under our banner, a radical stand.
SECOND COMRADE Bastard. Not an ounce of principle in him.
THIRD COMRADE Like all the rest.
FIRST COMRADE And every time it's because of some woman —
FOURTH COMRADE Obviously thinks no end of herself.
THIRD COMRADE Look at her! God, how graceful she is!
FIRST COMRADE She'll never understand where she belongs.
SECOND COMRADE Who is she, anyway?
FIRST COMRADE Just another working-class girl.
FIRST COMRADE No. She's definitely a more delicate morsel. She'll be a clerk — (*grins*)
THIRD COMRADE (*laughs*)
FOURTH COMRADE When do we start?
THIRD COMRADE (*suddenly stops laughing*)

The Italian Evening 27

MARTIN When I give you the signal. When *I* give it! (*stands up, goes over to where people are dancing and watches them; the band is playing a waltz, a few couples stop dancing, among them Councilman Ammetsberger*)
COUNCILMAN AMMETSBERGER Not a bad idea, eh?
ENGELBERT A splendid idea!
COUNCILMAN AMMETSBERGER I knew an informal gathering like this would bring we republicans closer together.
KRANZ (*slightly tipsy*) I'm just happy we didn't allow ourselves to be intimidated by those fucking reactionaries and that we just brushed aside our dear landlord's total lack of principle. That shows real character.
COUNCILMAN AMMETSBERGER A splendid idea!
ENGELBERT A propaganda coup!
KRANZ Those goddam fascists would be really cheesed off if they could see how at home we republicans feel here. They'll not get me to move that soon! (*staggers a little*)
ENGELBERT Where have those fascists got to?
BETZ I heard some talk of night maneuvers.
ENGELBERT Rather them than me!
KRANZ Cheers.
COUNCILMAN AMMETSBERGER All these childish games with small-bore rifles.
BETZ But people say they also have machine —
COUNCILMAN AMMETSBERGER (*interrupts him*) Talk, nothing but talk! Chin up, comrades! May I introduce my wife, my better half.
KRANZ Very pleased to meet you.
ENGELBERT How do you do.
BETZ We know each other by sight.
COUNCILMAN AMMETSBERGER'S BETTER HALF (*gives a timid smile*)
COUNCILMAN AMMETSBERGER You do? Where did you meet then?
BETZ I once saw you out walking with her.
COUNCILMAN AMMETSBERGER Me? With her? But we never go out together.
BETZ Well I did. It must have been just before Christmas —

COUNCILMAN AMMETSBERGER Of course! It was her birthday. The one day in the year when I let her go to the cinema with me. (*smiles and gives her cheek a playful pinch*) She's called Adele. Today's an exception, a big exception. Adele doesn't like appearing in public, she prefers it at home. (*grins*) She's a little homebody.
KRANZ (*to Adele*) Home sweet home. Home is where the heart is. Our republic is founded on family values. Oh give me a home . . . (*staggers off back to his beer humming*)
BETZ What an old rascal.
ENGELBERT (*to Adele*) May I have the pleasure?
COUNCILMAN AMMETSBERGER No thank you. Adele shouldn't dance. She's all perspiring.
ENGELBERT (*dances with a fifteen-year-old girl*)
ADELE (*timidly*) Alphonse!
COUNCILMAN AMMETSBERGER What?
ADELE I'm not perspiring.
COUNCILMAN AMMETSBERGER Please leave that to me.
ADELE Well why shouldn't I dance?
COUNCILMAN AMMETSBERGER But you can't dance.
ADELE Me? Yes I can dance.
COUNCILMAN AMMETSBERGER Since when?
ADELE I've always been able to dance.
COUNCILMAN AMMETSBERGER You've never been able to dance! Not even as a young girl. Just you remember that. And remember my position. I don't want my wife showing me up. (*lights a cigar; pause*)
ADELE Alphonse, why did you say I don't like appearing in public? I'd like to go out with you more often. — Why did you say that?
COUNCILMAN AMMETSBERGER Because.
(*pause*)
ADELE I know you've a public position to keep up —
COUNCILMAN AMMETSBERGER And that's why you should stay quiet.
ADELE You're always showing me up in the wrong light. You said I don't go out with you —
COUNCILMAN AMMETSBERGER You see!

ADELE (*testily*) What do I see?
COUNCILMAN AMMETSBERGER That you're no match for me.
(*silence*)
ADELE I feel I don't want to go anywhere, ever again.
COUNCILMAN AMMETSBERGER Excellent idea! (*turns his back on her; to Betz*) My wife, hm? (*grins and shakes his finger playfully at her*) When you go to a woman don't forget your whip.
BETZ That's by Nietzsche.
COUNCILMAN AMMETSBERGER I don't care who it's by. She follows my every command, to the letter. A glorious spot this! Those ancient trunks, and the air — all that ozone! (*breathes in deeply*)
BETZ The wonder of nature.
COUNCILMAN AMMETSBERGER The wonder of creation — there's nothing more glorious. I can appreciate that better because I come from farming stock. If you look up to the sky you feel so tiny — the eternal stars! What are we compared with them?
BETZ Nothing.
COUNCILMAN AMMETSBERGER Nothing. Everything's in the best of taste in God's creation.
BETZ Yes, well, everything's relative.
(*silence*)
COUNCILMAN AMMETSBERGER You know what, Betz, I've bought myself a piece of land.
BETZ Where?
COUNCILMAN AMMETSBERGER Almost an acre. With a clearing. — Look at it this way, old friend: the world has room for a couple of billion people, why shouldn't a tiny little piece of that great big world belong to me? —
FIRST COMRADE (*happens to have overheard*) A fine Marxist!
(*silence*)
COUNCILMAN AMMETSBERGER What did he say?
BETZ Just ignore him.
ADELE He said, "A fine Marxist."
COUNCILMAN AMMETSBERGER You say that to my face? Just like that? Oh great!
ADELE I only said what he said.

COUNCILMAN AMMETSBERGER Who? The insolence of these young whippersnappers! Just look at them! (*points to Martin and his comrades*) Call themselves young — not one of them has danced! Opposition and nothing but opposition. Revolts and that kind of thing. Splinter groups. Authority, that's what we need. We ought to — (*he is about to go back to his table, but pauses when he sees that Martin and his comrades are quietly discussing something in a group; he tries to hear what is being said, then suddenly strides up to Martin*) What did you say then? A fine Marxist, was that what you said?

MARTIN I didn't actually say it, but I could have.

COUNCILMAN AMMETSBERGER And what would you have meant by it, if you had said it?

MARTIN We'll talk about that later. (*walks away*)

(*The band plays a chord, followed by a gong*)

ENGELBERT (*on the podium*) Ladies and gentlemen. Comrades. I am happy to announce there is a delightful surprise in store for you, a rare artistic treat. Frau Hinterberger, the wife of our treasurer, has very kindly agreed to give us the pleasure of her alto voice! (*cheers and applause*) Silence, please. Frau Hinterberger.

FRAU HINTERBERGER (*comes onto the podium and is greeted with applause*) I'm going to sing a ballad by Karl Loewe: Heinrich der Vogler.

(*She sings the ballad; loud applause, only Martin and his comrades refuse to join in again; the dancing continues*)

LENI (*to Karl*) That was lovely. I'm very musical, you know.

KARL I'd already noticed that.

LENI How did you guess?

KARL From your dancing. You have a truly incredible sensitivity to rhythm.

LENI But that's not just me. it depends on the man I'm dancing with as well.

KARL So you don't regret coming to the party with me?

LENI (*with a smile*) Now don't you start getting political again! — Promise me you won't, ever. Word of honor?

KARL It's not that simple.

LENI Why not?

KARL Well, you see, I only like to give my word of honor when I know I can keep it. It's much easier to break a word of honor than to keep it.
LENI If you give me your word of honor, I'll give you mine —
KARL You?
LENI A woman hasn't much to give, but when she does give what she has, she makes a man a king.
MARTIN (*to Karl*) Karl, could I have a word —
KARL Of course. (*to Leni*) Excuse me. (*to Martin*) What is it?
MARTIN You promised Anna you wouldn't dance. I'm just pointing out that you've broken your political word of honor for the sake of amusement.
KARL (*getting worked up*) Have I now?
MARTIN You have. And you even promised me that when the great ideological debate starts here —
KARL (*interrupting him*) Don't get on your moral high horse again!
MARTIN You've prostituted your honor once again.
KARL Do you mean that seriously?
MARTIN Yes. You unprincipled bohemian —
(*silence*)
KARL (*with a malicious smile*) Where's Anna, Martin?
MARTIN Why d'you ask?
KARL Is she going to turn up soon?
MARTIN Did you see her?
KARL Yes.
MARTIN Alone or in company?
KARL In company.
MARTIN (*smiling*) That's OK then.
KARL You think so?
MARTIN Yes.
(*silence*)
KARL (*with a grin*) Honi soit qui mal y pense.
MARTIN What's all that about?
KARL (*gloating*) That's French.
(*silence*)
MARTIN I don't hold it against you, I feel sorry for you. It's just sad to see you wasting your abilities. All we get from you is

excuses. You're not a real man, just a moral cripple — (*turns on his heel*)
(*A chord from the band followed by the gong*)
ENGELBERT (*on the podium*) Ladies and gentlemen. Comrades. Another delightful surprise in our program. Our series of artistic performances continues with a top-quality ballet danced by the charming Leimsieder twins. Title: "The flower and the butterfly."
THE CHARMING LEIMSIEDER TWINS (*thirteen; come onto the podium, to thunderous applause*)
COUNCILMAN AMMETSBERGER Bravo Leimsieder!
THE CHARMING LEIMSIEDER TWINS (*their dance is pretentious kitsch. Suddenly a piercing whistle is heard from Martin's part of the room; the charming twins give a start but carry on with the dance, though a bit uncertainly. Those who are enjoying it give Martin outraged stares — then another whistle is heard, even more piercing than the first.*)
KRANZ (*shouting*) Quiet, for Christ's sake! Which one of you's whistling, you young hooligans? Load of guttersnipes!
ENGELBERT If you don't like it there nothing to stop you leaving.
SHOUTS Out! Out!
(*commotion*)
THE CHARMING LEIMSIEDER TWINS (*burst into loud tears*)
FIRST COMRADE (*thumps the table with his fist*) We don't want an infant's ballet here.
KRANZ I told you, shut your face!
SECOND COMRADE You shut yours!
AN AUNT Look, now you've made the children cry! How can you be so heartless!?
THIRD COMRADE Bourgeois claptrap!
FOURTH COMRADE Bourgeois trip-trap!
COUNCILMAN AMMETSBERGER I've had enough of this.
COMRADES (*jeer*)
COUNCILMAN AMMETSBERGER You'll soon find out who you're dealing with!
COMRADES (*jeer*)
COUNCILMAN AMMETSBERGER We know how to deal with your kind!

The Italian Evening 33

THIRD COMRADE Da-da-da-da, here comes the cavalry!
THE AUNT Young people nowadays!
FOURTH COMRADE A fine Marxist!
COMRADES (*chanting*) A fine Marxist! A fine Marxist! A fine Marxist! A fine Marxist!
COUNCILMAN AMMETSBERGER Who? Me? I knew the Communist Manifesto by heart when you were still in diapers, you young louts. (*whistle*)
THE AUNT We were enjoying an artistic performance and you barbarians are just spoiling it.
FOURTH COMRADE Artistic performance my ass!
THIRD COMRADE The flower and the butterfly!
FIRST COMRADE Crap! Crap! Crap!
KRANZ Oh you philistines! (*falls under the table, drunk*)
ENGELBERT See what you've done now!? Children in tears! Aren't you ashamed of yourselves? Have you any idea of all the love that's gone into rehearsing this? For weeks comrade Leimsieder and his wife have sacrificed every minute of their free time so we can enjoy this artistic experience.
COMRADE FROM OUTSIDE (*from Magdeburg, Party headquarters*) He'd have been better employed sacrificing every minute of his free time strengthening the effective power of our organization.
(*deathly silence; great surprise at the strange accent*)
COINCILMAN AMMETSBERGER Aha, a Prussian —
(*storm of protest*)
FRAU DVORAK Don't spoil our evening!
MARTIN This kind of evening ought to be spoiled!
COMRADE FROM OUTSIDE Comrades!
MARTIN I'm the one who's speaking. — Comrades, while we're putting on family parties with children's ballet, the right wing are putting on military night maneuvers with machine guns!
COMRADE FROM OUTSIDE Fellow Party members, can't you see how they are denying, mocking, exploiting the proletariat? Worse than ever! And what do you do?
MARTIN (*interrupting him*) And what do you do? Put on Italian Evenings! Have you forgotten what one of our leaders said? Oh, if only every proletarian delighted in republican —

COMRADE FROM OUTSIDE (*interrupts him*) Revolutionary! In revolutionary activity. We make the following demand —
COUNCILMAN AMMETSBERGER You make no demands here!
MARTIN We demand an immediate extraordinary meeting of the committee to discuss the proposal to —
COMRADE FROM OUTSIDE — arm the comrades with small-bore rifles!
KRANZ Shut your face! Goddam Prussian!
SHOUTS Out! Out!
COMRADE FROM OUTSIDE Fellow comrades!
MARTIN I'm the one who's speaking, for Christ's sake! You're getting me all mixed up. We both want the same thing, but we'll get nowhere this way. Let the local leadership speak.
COUNCILMAN AMMETSBERGER Comrades! It's an outrage. An outsider has the audacity to disrupt our celebration. Make little children cry. — Comrades, what Martin is demanding is impracticable. We're not going to follow the example of the right wing. No guns for us, but anyone who poses a serious threat to our democratic republic will be beaten off!
MARTIN And what with?
COUNCILMAN AMMETSBERGER All the bayonets international right-wing extremism can throw at us will simply smash to pieces on our implacable determination to preserve peace!
SEVENTH COMRADE (*laughs in his face*)
COUNCILMAN AMMETSBERGER Look at them! That's what you get when you deny the power of moral persuasion!
FIRST COMRADE Just empty phrases, you apostle of humanism, you!
COUNCILMAN AMMETSBERGER They are not empty phrases! We just don't want to see any more weapons. My wife lost two brothers in the war.
FOURTH COMRADE And in the next war it'll be us, me and Stiegler and him there and him there.
KRANZ (*imitating him*) And me there and me there and me there!
COUNCILMAN AMMETSBERGER There are to be no more wars! It's a crime and we're going to stop it happening. I'll see to that.
MARTIN Just as you did in 1914.

The Italian Evening 35

COUNCILMAN AMMETSBERGER The situation was different then.
COMRADE FROM OUTSIDE The same old story, the same old story.
COUNCILMAN AMMETSBERGER Where were you in 1914? In kindergarten!
COMRADE FROM OUTSIDE And you? In 1914 you were boasting of the deeds of your ancestors, which is more than we can do!
MARTIN Comrades!! If we go on like this tomorrow morning we'll wake up in the Holy Mussolinian Roman Empire.
COMRADE FROM OUTSIDE Fellow Party members!!
KRANZ (*beside himself*) Come on, let's throw this mucking Prussian loudmouth out. Out! Out! Out!
MARTIN Silence!! What's Prussian got to do with anything. — Let's get to the point. The long and short of it is, this kind of Italian Evening deserves to be disrupted, radically disrupted!
COUNCILMAN AMMETSBERGER Point of order! In line with our constitution I demand that comrade Martin be excluded immediately.
ENGELBERT Hear, hear!
COUNCILMAN AMMETSBERGER The reason: uncomradely behavior.
MARTIN Great! Well done! Come on. (*off with his comrades*)
COUNCILMAN AMMETSBERGER We'll have no splits at our Italian Evening, comrades. I've been looking forward to it for two weeks and I'm not going to be split. Music! Sit down everyone.

SCENE SIX

Outside Lehninger's inn. Martin and his comrades are just leaving the Italian Evening. On the right a public convenience.

MARTIN So I'm excluded. For uncomradely behavior. It's enough to make you laugh.
(*silence*)
SECOND COMRADE Where to then?
MARTIN My place.
COMRADE FROM OUTSIDE Let's get to work. There's not a minute to lose.
MARTIN The bourgeoisie'll soon be retreating back into the fortress of dictatorship.
COMRADE FROM OUTSIDE Be prepared!
(*silence*)
MARTIN (*speaks quietly, suspiciously*) Who's that anyway?
FIRST COMRADE I don't know him.
THIRD COMRADE Completely unknown to me.
(*They go into the convenience.*)
COMRADE FROM OUTSIDE (*following them*) I'm from Magdeburg, comrades.
MARTIN'S VOICE (*from inside the convenience*) From Magdeburg is it? So you are from Prussia. Well I've just one thing to say to you and that's that I'm the official leader here and we have this convention that the appointed leader leads the operation and no one else. Whether they're from Magdeburg or not. (*reappears with his comrades*)
(*silence*)
MARTIN (*to the First Comrade*) Do you think daubing His Majesty's monument was appropriate in the circumstances?
SECOND COMRADE (*with ironic formality, not in dialect*) We took the liberty of giving His Majesty's monument a coat of red paint.
MARTIN Who's we?
SECOND COMRADE Me.
FOURTH COMRADE And me.

MARTIN So. You as well. It was totally stupid, of course. Or don't you agree?
COMRADE FROM OUTSIDE Desecrating a monument is nothing but a childish prank. Forget about dynasties that have been thrown out, you guys. Put your energies into making sure no one raises any monuments to the capitalists.
(*silence*)
MARTIN (*talks quietly with his comrades, then turns to the Comrade From Outside*) Do you know what I think? I think you're an agent provocateur —
COMRADE FROM OUTSIDE (*horrified*) Comrade!
MARTIN That's all we need, agents provocateurs from — Magdeburg. (*turns his back on him*)
COMRADE FROM OUTSIDE It's enough to drive you to despair.
MARTIN You still here? Are you still here? (*goes up to him threateningly*)
COMRADE FROM OUTSIDE (*leaves rapidly*)
KARL (*coming out of the inn with Leni*) Everything's at sixes and sevens in there.
THIRD COMRADE Great!
LENI Everyone's leaving. The party mood's all down the pan.
SIXTH COMRADE Then it's where it belongs.
KARL Martin, I've come to beg your forgiveness.
MARTIN What for?
KARL For breaking my word of honor. I've thought this through and it was wrong of me, but in fact it only appeared to be wrong, I only appeared to break my word.
MARTIN What on earth am I supposed to make of that?
KARL I had to dance, you see. I'd promised your Anna that I'd try and convert that girl over there to our ideas, and with a girl like that you have to make some concessions, work your way round gradually to —
MARTIN It's always girls you convert —
KARL Each to his own. I belong to an older generation than you and it does make a difference, even though there's only five years between us, five years of war —

MARTIN History doesn't give a shit about individuals and their pathetic little lives, it just marches straight over them, and it's marching forwards.
KARL I agree with you entirely there.
MARTIN You'd be some use if we could believe you, but we can't. You've never really grown up.
KARL It's all right for you, your sex-life is straightforward. God, how I envy you sometimes.
MARTIN And I feel sorry for you. I've tried, I've tried I don't know how many times, but this is it. Your further presence in the group is no longer required.
KARL (*sketches a bow*) As you wish. I' sorry. (*exits with Leni; the comrades leave too*)
ANNA (*enters*)
MARTIN Anna!
ANNA You gave me a surprise there.
MARTIN Me?
ANNA I thought you were someone else —
MARTIN You did?
ANNA Just now you looked so different. Almost a stranger.
MARTIN (*almost a mocking tone*) Did I now? — Did you get anything out of him?
ANNA Several things.
MARTIN For example?
ANNA For example I learned that the fascists are going to break up our Italian Evening —
MARTIN (*interrupting*) In the first place it's not our Italian Evening and in the second place their Italian Evening has already been broken up. I saw to it personally.
ANNA Already?
MARTIN More about that later. What else?
ANNA The fascists want to beat everyone up in there.
MARTIN I'm all for that! Just what that committee needs! The tactics of those petty bourgeois betray the working class and it would do them good to feel the consequences themselves — physically. We younger ones should leave them to it and set our own course.

ANNA I wouldn't do that.
MARTIN What do you mean by that?
ANNA I wouldn't do that. I'd help them. At least they're closer to us than the others.
MARTIN You don't say.
ANNA Councilman Ammetsberger might deserve a good hiding, but there are others there who are probably trying their honest best —
MARTIN (*ironically*) You think so?
ANNA And when all's said and done, conflicts among us have nothing to do with outsiders. They're our conflicts.
MARTIN (*with spite*) I can well believe that's your personal point of view.
ANNA Please don't speak to me like that.
(*silence*)
MARTIN What else?
ANNA Nothing else. The fascists are fuming, that's all. Some statue is supposed to have been vandalized this evening.
MARTIN Yes, that was that idiot Stiegler —
ANNA Martin!
MARTIN (*surprised*) Huh?
ANNA You'd let the others in there get beaten up just because one of us daubed the statue with paint? I think that's cowardly. It's not worthy of us. It's unjust — (*breaks off as she notices Martin is staring in fascination at her neck*)
(*silence*)
MARTIN (*softly*) What's that bruise there?
ANNA Where?
MARTIN There.
ANNA There? That's a bruise —
(*silence*)
ANNA It'll be all blue tomorrow.
MARTIN It will, will it?
ANNA He was a bit rough.
MARTIN (*somewhat uncertain*) He was rough, was he —
ANNA That's what men are like, all of them —
(*silence*)

MARTIN Look at me.
ANNA (*doesn't look at him.*)
MARTIN Why won't you look at me?
ANNA Because I can't.
MARTIN Why can't you look at me just now? And don't give me that stupid look, for Christ's sake!
(*silence*)
ANNA I suddenly got this funny feeling just now —
MARTIN How do you mean?
ANNA You asking me to pick up a fascist, any fascist — you of all people —
MARTIN This new feeling —
ANNA It wasn't new, it was an old feeling —
MARTIN Primitive sentimentality! You know I can't stand it. We've put these problems behind us, what's the point of bringing them up again. Don't put yourself under any illusions, I beg you.
ANNA There you go again. Please don't talk to me in that stilted way.
(*silence*)
MARTIN Anna — he was rough with you was he, your fascist? —
ANNA Yes.
MARTIN Very rough?
ANNA Not specially.
(*silence*)
MARTIN But he was rough. — Yes, perhaps it is beneath us, after all.
ANNA What is?
MARTIN Letting that committee in there get beaten up because of His Royal Highness's red face — by those fascists.
ANNA You see!
MARTIN What am I supposed to see? I don't see anything, anything at all! We're just going not going to let those fascists have their little triumph, that's all. Come on. (*exits with Anna*)
KARL (*enters with Leni. Both seem to be rather depressed. They sit on the bench next to the public convenience.*)
LENI You haven't said anything for ages. Why not?
KARL Because I'm sick at heart, that's why.

LENI But it's not your fault that Italian Evening ended up on a sour note.
KARL Thank you for that. (*gives her hand a squeeze then buries his head in his hands*)
(*silence*)
LENI That comrade of yours, Martin, he reminds me of someone I used to know. It was no good talking to him either, the only thing that meant anything to him was his motorbike. He won lots of races too and I just got in the way of his practice. Don't be sad —
KARL I don't feel I want to live anymore.
LENI Why ever not?
KARL I'm too keen-sighted. I can see the way the world's going and I think to myself if only I were a few years younger I could play an active part in improving things — but I'm a moral cripple. And tired.
LENI You're just talking yourself into believing that.
KARL Never really grown up! Never a real man playing a real man's part in the fight against fascism.
LENI Don't get depressed.
KARL I think there must be a curse on me.
LENI No there isn't.
KARL (*standing up*) Yes there is.
(*silence*)
KARL (*sits down again*)
LENI Do you believe in God?
KARL (*says nothing*)
LENI There is a God and that means there's the possibility of salvation.
KARL If only I knew who put the curse on me.
LENI Let me save you.
KARL You? me?
LENI I have four thousand marks. We can set up a grocery store —
KARL We?
LENI Out where my uncle lives —
KARL We?
LENI Me and you.
(*silence*)

KARL Cash?
LENI Cash.
(*silence*)
KARL And what's your idea? Is it a marriage partnership you have in mind? You don't want to throw yourself away on that.
LENI How can you say such hard-hearted things? I know you through and through, even though I've only known you for a short time. (*throws her arms round him; big scene with a long kiss*)
KARL I always dreamed of being saved by a woman, but I just couldn't get round to believing it — I've got very embittered, you know?
LENI (*gives him a kiss on the forehead*) I know. The world is full of envy.

SCENE SEVEN

In the garden of Lehninger's inn. The Republican Italian Evening has now been completely broken up, only the committee is left sitting under the Chinese lanterns: Councilman Ammetsberger with Adele, Betz, Engelbert, and Kranz. The last has his head on a table and is snoring. It is already getting toward midnight and Adele is shivering as there is a chilly wind blowing.

BETZ What now?
ENGELBERT Home?
COUNCILMAN AMMETSBERGER (*suddenly standing up*) No, never! Over my dead body. We're going to go through with our Italian Evening. No surrender, comrades, we're staying put — until closing time! *sits down again.*
ENGELBERT Hear, hear!
COUNCILMAN AMMETSBERGER (*lights a cigar somewhat nervously*)
KRANZ (*wakes up and yawns expansively; to Betz*) Hey, I've just had a fantastic dream.
BETZ A pleasant one?
KRANZ Very. I dreamed of this republic, and it was such a complete republic even the monarchists were secret republicans.
BETZ Ah, what you have there is what we call wish fulfillment.
KRANZ Oh, really?
ENGELBERT How about a round of cards?
COUNCILMAN AMMETSBERGER Cards?
ENGELBERT With a little kitty.
KRANZ Ten pfennigs a round!
COUNCILMAN AMMETSBERGER Perhaps that would be the most sensible thing to do.
ENGELBERT I have a deck. (*sits at a table with the Councilman Ammetsberger and Kranz under the brightest of the Chinese lanterns, shuffles and deals*)
Off we go then.
BETZ (*kibitzes*)
KRANZ Play.
COUNCILMAN AMMETSBERGER Play too.

KRANZ Pass.
ENGELBERT Five more.
COUNCILMAN AMMETSBERGER Ten more.
ENGELBERT Pass.
KRANZ And the light shineth in darkness — (*leads*)
(*The wind is getting stronger*)
ADELE (*stands up, shivering*) When are we going to go?
COUNCILMAN AMMETSBERGER I've already said. Clubs.
ADELE I'll catch cold —
COUNCILMAN AMMETSBERGER I'd be sorry about that. Hearts.
KRANZ And hearts.
ENGELBERT And hearts.
BETZ (*comes up to Adele*) We're staying until closing time, Frau Ammetsberger.
ADELE And when is closing time?
BETZ Two o'clock.
ADELE And what is it now?
BETZ Getting on for twelve.
ADELE Oh, God!
COUNCILMAN AMMETSBERGER (*to Betz*) Leave her alone please.
(*silence*)
ADELE I'll catch my death of cold.
BETZ Or pneumonia. (*pause*) If you're going to die, then dying for an ideal is the best way to go.
ADELE I can't think of an ideal I would want to die for.
BETZ (*with a faint smile*) Not even the ideals for which your husband gives of himself so self-sacrificingly?
ADELE He gives of himself?
BETZ Day and night.
ADELE Well you should know.
BETZ Everything's relative of course.
(*silence*)
ADELE A man who doesn't have such publicly proclaimed ideals is much nicer to his family, believe you me. I'm talking in purely human terms when I say that, of course. You're an intelligent man, Herr Betz, I've noticed that already.

COUNCILMAN AMMETSBERGER What have you two got to talk about that's so enthralling?
BETZ You.
COUNCILMAN AMMETSBERGER Really? Couldn't you find a more rewarding subject?
ADELE (*sharply*) Alphonse!
COUNCILMAN AMMETSBERGER What's the matter now?
ADELE I'd like a ham sandwich.
COUNCILMAN AMMETSBERGER You've already had two. I'd have thought that was sufficient. (*lights another cigar*)
ADELE If you can smoke your cigars —
COUNCILMAN AMMETSBERGER (*interrupts her*) Oh you're impossible! Yuck! It's not drawing properly. That's your fault, you begrudge me every little pleasure. (*throws the cigar away in fury*) That cigar's impossible.
ADELE (*getting up*) I'd like to go home now.
COUNCILMAN AMMETSBERGER You're just doing it to spite me.
ADELE I'm going —
COUNCILMAN AMMETSBERGER And I'm staying.
ADELE Please come home!
COUNCILMAN AMMETSBERGER No! You're staying here I say!
ADELE No, I have to get up at six again to wash your shirts —
COUNCILMAN AMMETSBERGER You're staying, I tell you.
ADELE I'll catch my death here —
COUNCILMAN AMMETSBERGER You're staying and that's that. Understood?
ADELE (*sits down again with a pained smile on her face*)
COUNCILMAN AMMETSBERGER Play.
ENGELBERT Pass.
KRANZ Play too.
ENGELBERT How many?
KRANZ Sixty-five.
COUNCILMAN AMMETSBERGER Don't make me laugh! I'll take the lot. Yes, the lot! And it's my lead. (*leads and wins the game quickly and roars with laughter*)
(*silence*)
BETZ But why don't you go home by yourself then?

ADELE Because he won't let me go by myself.

BETZ Won't let you? Won't let you go even if you go by yourself? But he's no right to dictate to you. Good Lord, that puts him in a different light, although I was expecting it. — My old comrade Alphonse Ammetsberger — thirty-five years. — Yes, yes, it must be old age. I wonder if I've changed that much as well?

COUNCILMAN AMMETSBERGER (*to Betz*) Please, Betz, leave her in peace.

INNKEEPER (*enters; very drunk and staggers as he waves to them; no one pays any attention to him; he grins*) Boycott me then, go on, boycott me. I don't care anymore, I won't be shedding any tears over you. The reactionaries are much better customers anyway. What do your young people drink? Nothing but soda water. A nice party you Republicans are! Soda water!

KRANZ Shut up.

INNKEEPER (*suddenly going dreamy*) It's the john I'm thinking of. In the old days, you see, the scribblings on the wall were just obscene jokes, then during the war it was patriotic appeals and now it's political slogans. I tell you, Germany won't be her old self again until we get back to dirty jokes —

KRANZ You shut your foul mouth, you filthy swine.

INNKEEPER Pardon? — Heinrich, you're the only sensible person round here, what did that gentleman over there say?

BETZ He said you should shut your face.

INNKEEPER Did he now? What a naughty boy. — By the way, my dear friends, I have a delightful piece of news for you

KRANZ We're not your dear friends.

INNKEEPER What did he say?

BETZ He said we're not your dear friends.

INNKEEPER Is that what he said? Well then. Gentlemen, it is my privilege to make a gratifying announcement: you are surrounded, gentlemen, completely surrounded.

COUNCILMAN AMMETSBERGER (*looks up*)

BETZ Who's surrounded?

INNKEEPER You are, gentlemen.

ENGELBERT What do you mean?

The Italian Evening 47

INNKEEPER I've just been informed, gentlemen, that the fascists intend to beat you up.
COUNCILMAN AMMETSBERGER (*stands up*)
INNKEEPER The fascist gentlemen maintain that you gentlemen here have bedaubed the statue.
COUNCILMAN AMMETSBERGER What statue?
INNKEEPER The statue of His Majesty.
ENGELBERT No idea what you're on about.
INNKEEPER The fascists are filled with rightful fury and intend to restore the honor of His Majesty. With blood! Three cheers!
KRANZ Jesus wept!
INNKEEPER It's no good denying it, gentlemen. All the evidence is against you. Interrogation and that kind of thing. The verdict is guilty.
COUNCILMAN AMMETSBERGER Lies! A pack of lies! No one here's been daubing paint on His Majesty and that's the truth.
INNKEEPER (*raises his glass*) Your very good health. (*empties it*) (*silence*)
BETZ Josef, who told you we're going to be beaten up?
INNKEEPER Anna. Martin's Anna.
COUNCILMAN AMMETSBERGER (*sharply*) Martin? Very interesting.
INNKEEPER In confidence. A lady's honor.
KRANZ I don't know what to think now.
ENGELBERT It must be a mistake. Looking at it logically —
COUNCILMAN AMMETSBERGER (*sharply*) Or treachery! We have a clear conscience.
INNKEEPER Clear or not, the fists are going to fly now, gentlemen.
KRANZ You Judas, you!
INNKEEPER (*in a whine*) But I'm not a Judas at all. I've always been loyal to you, deep down inside, even after the revolution. The world's turned upside down. In the old days Sundays were just for fun and if there was a bit of a ruckus now and then it was over some fat-assed woman, never over these goddam politics. It's an unhealthy sign gentlemen.
KRANZ (*raises his hand to speak*) I'd like to propose a motion. I would like to argue that we should keep our calm, stay here and

wait and see. We'll win all the arguments; we're in the right and we're innocent, radically innocent.
ENGELBERT Hear, hear!
BETZ (*to Kranz*) You're forgetting our aggressive drive again —
KRANZ You what?
INNKEEPER It'll come to blows.
BETZ I'm speaking from a more general point of view. By nature man is naturally cruel — one has to face up to the truth, my friend.
INNKEEPER How very true.
COUNCILMAN AMMETSBERGER Comrades! In the face of destiny man, whether monarchist or republican, is no more than a reed in the wind. There are times when even the boldest of us has to bow before the voice of reason, even if it goes against the grain. Comrades, it would be a poor general who led his brigades to certain defeat. With that in mind, I hereby declare our Italian Evening closed. *Force majeure* — I bow to superior force. Where's my hat?
BETZ I'm staying.
COUNCILMAN AMMETSBERGER What d'you mean?
BETZ I have come to a somewhat different opinion —
COUNCILMAN AMMETSBERGER I shouldn't have thought there was a different opinion to come to.
BETZ Oh, you don't do you? We have a completely clear conscience as far as the soiled statue is concerned.
ENGELBERT Quite right!
BETZ Consequently I think it's not right of us simply to run away.
COUNCILMAN AMMETSBERGER Not not right, sensible! We all know these fascists outnumber us and that means there's no extremes they won't go to. Where's my hat?
BETZ I'm staying, even if they do beat me up.
(*silence*)
COUNCILMAN AMMETSBERGER (*giving him a mocking stare*) Aha, a political masochist. Well I hope you enjoy it.
BETZ Thank you.
COUNCILMAN AMMETSBERGER (*with a grin*) God, how heroic.
BETZ Better beaten up than a coward.
COUNCILMAN AMMETSBERGER You think so?

The Italian Evening

ADELE I think so too.
COUNCILMAN AMMETSBERGER What you think is neither here nor there.
ADELE But that's still what I think.
COUNCILMAN AMMETSBERGER (*goes over to her slowly; in an undertone*) What you think is neither here nor there, understood?!
ADELE I'm only giving my views.
COUNCILMAN AMMETSBERGER Your views are neither here nor there.
ADELE (*with venom*) Do you think so?
COUNCILMAN AMMETSBERGER Don't show me up, right?
ADELE Of course not.
COUNCILMAN AMMETSBERGER (*pinches her*)
ADELE Ouch! Ouch!
COUNCILMAN AMMETSBERGER Will you keep yourself under control?!
ADELE Ouch! Alphonse! Ouch!
COUNCILMAN AMMETSBERGER Keep yourself under control! Keep yourself —
ADELE (*tears herself away with a screech*) Ouch! — You and your ideals!
COUNCILMAN AMMETSBERGER Oh, you're impossible, woman!
ADELE Oh, you're impossible! A proletarian on the outside, a capitalist on the inside. These gentlemen here should find out what you're really like. He's been exploiting me. Me! For thirty years, thirty years! (*bursts into tears*)
COUNCILMAN AMMETSBERGER (*with his hand over his eyes*) Adele! Adele —
(*silence*)
COUNCILMAN AMMETSBERGER (*slowly takes his hands away from his eyes*) Where's my hat?
INNKEEPER (*gets up ponderously*) Hat or no hat, you're surrounded and nothing's going to change that — (*burps and staggers off*)
ADELE (*suddenly grins*)
COUNCILMAN AMMETSBERGER It's no laughing matter!

ADELE When I look at you like that I find it funny, really funny, the way you block the way for younger people — (*starts sobbing again*)
COUNCILMAN AMMETSBERGER Stop crying!
ADELE It's just nerves.
KRANZ Female logic. Typical!
ADELE (*crying*) If you hadn't had the young men chucked out no one would dare come and get us. Now there's only the old cripples left —
ENGELBERT Oh, come on now.
COUNCILMAN AMMETSBERGER Oh my God!
ADELE You leave God out of it.
KRANZ There's no such thing as God. (*silence. raises his hand*) I'd like to propose a motion. I would like to argue that it was as you might say hasty to exclude Martin just like that, and his supporters too — he has quite a lot of support, strong support, could be worse, and he wasn't all that wrong, as you might say —
COUNCILMAN AMMETSBERGER You think so?
KRANZ If we had small-bore rifles like these fascists then we wouldn't have to sit here and get beaten up for something we didn't so, we could defend ourselves — *defend* ourselves — that makes sense, doesn't it?
ENGELBERT Sense or no sense, according to the constitution we had to exclude Martin.
KRANZ Sense or no sense, I don't give a shit for the constitution.
ENGELBERT Hear, hear.
KRANZ It's out of date, that's what the constitution is.
COUNCILMAN AMMETSBERGER So suddenly?
KRANZ I would like to propose an official motion that Comrade Martin's overhasty exclusion be rescinded.
COUNCILMAN AMMETSBERGER Rescinded?
KRANZ Yes, rescinded!
COUNCILMAN AMMETSBERGER (*looks round questioningly*) What's the feeling?
BETZ Yes.
ENGELBERT Hmm.
COUNCILMAN AMMETSBERGER (*to Engelbert, softly*) Yes or no?

(silence)
ENGELBERT Yes.
(silence)
COUNCILMAN AMMETSBERGER Where's my hat?
ADELE *(hands him his hat)* There.
COUNCILMAN AMMETSBERGER *(puts it on and pulls it down over his forehead; in a toneless voice)* I'll withdraw from public life — I'll not go out any more — at most to the bowls or the choir —
ADELE At last, Alphonse.
(trumpet fanfare)
MAJOR *(in the uniform of Germany's former colonial army; enters quickly with two fascists, stops right in front of the Councilman Ammetsberger and gives him a fierce stare)*
(silence)
MAJOR I already have the dubious honour of your acquaintance.
COUNCILMAN AMMETSBERGER *(nods apathetically)*
MAJOR I can tell from the shifty look in your eye and the guilty expressions on the faces of your accomplices that you have already guessed the reason for my presence here.
ENGELBERT We're innocent! Radically innocent!
MAJOR Silence! You've just given yourselves away.
(deathly hush)
MAJOR *(roars)* Silence! We'll soon sort you lot out. Red scum!
BETZ But everything's relative —
MAJOR Hold your tongue! We'll show you what's what, by Jove. Revenge for Strasbourg! We'll teach you to desecrate monuments — It strikes at our honor and blood is our honor!
BETZ Absolute bullshit.
MAJOR What?!
BETZ *(lights a cigar)*
MAJOR Put that cigar out!
BETZ If you insist — *(puts the cigar down)*
(silence.)
MAJOR Czernowitz.
CZERNOWITZ Yes, sir!
MAJOR Tell us now, how did your father deal with prisoners of war who tried passive resistance?

CZERNOWITZ He hammered bullets up their backsides, just like hammering nails into the wall, sir.
MAJOR (*to Betz*) Understood?
BETZ I don't have a backside —
MAJOR (*walks round Councilman Ammetsberger; suddenly bellows at him*) Attention! Sit down!
COUNCILMAN AMMETSBERGER (*sits down as if his mind is elsewhere*)
MAJOR (*waves one of the fascists over*)
FASCIST (*brings paper, pen and ink to Councilman Ammetsberger*)
MAJOR Good. You'll write what I dictate.
COUNCILMAN AMMETSBERGER (*obeys apathetically*)
MAJOR (*dictating*) I, Councilman Alphonse Ammetsberger and a red, hereby declare on my word of honor — Have you got that? On my word of honor? — that I am a complete —
COUNCILMAN AMMETSBERGER (*stops writing*)
MAJOR Write!
COUNCILMAN AMMETSBERGER (*starts writing again*)
MAJOR (*dictating*) — that I am a complete — scoundrel.
COUNCILMAN AMMETSBERGER (*stops again*)
MAJOR Is this going to take for ever?
COUNCILMAN AMMETSBERGER (*doesn't move*)
MAJOR If you don't jump to it you'll get six of the best. Now write.
COUNCILMAN AMMETSBERGER (*slowly bends forward over the paper; suddenly he starts whining and sobbing*) But I'm not a —
MAJOR Yes you are a scoundrel. You're a complete scoundrel.
ADELE Hey you! He's not a scoundrel, he's my husband. How dare you, you overdressed tailor's dummy. Leave the man in peace.
BETZ What right do you —
MAJOR (*interrupts him*) Hold your tongue.
ADELE Hold your own tongue. And you can take all that stuff off too. Don't you know the war's over, you clown? Why don't you donate your pension to the war invalids and do a decent day's work instead of going round interrupting ordinary people when they're having a garden party, you complete scoundrel, you?
MAJOR You foul-mouthed woman. Just you wait. There are forty good Germans waiting outside.

The Italian Evening 53

ADELE (*shouting after him*) That's my husband. Understood?
(*commotion outside the inn*)
MARTIN (*enters with Anna, followed by his comrades*)
ADELE Martin!
MARTIN At your service, Frau Ammetsberger. The coast is clear, gentlemen. I must tell you that the fascists were after *us*, me and my comrades, and not this committee here. And we're the kind of people who take responsibility for their own actions. However, allow me to announce that no one here has anything to fear any more. When the fascists saw us outside they quickly decided to redeploy. Radically redeploy! We've done it again.
COUNCILMAN AMMETSBERGER There you are. It just shows that all this talk of a serious threat to our democratic republic is nonsense. Comrades. As long as we have our Republican Defense Association and as long as I have the honor to be chairman of our local section, the Republic can sleep in peace.
MARTIN And good night to both of you.

Tales from the Vienna Woods

A Play in Seven Scenes

*There is nothing that gives one a
sense of infinity as much as stupidity.*

CHARACTERS
FAIRY KING
MARIANNE
OSCAR
MATHILDA
ALFRED
CAVALRY CAPTAIN
ERIC
HAVLICHEK
A LADY
FIRST AUNT
SECOND AUNT
IDA
CONGENITAL IDIOT
FATHER CONFESSOR
EMMA
THE AMERICAN
MC
GRANDMOTHER
MOTHER
DAUGHTER
GROWN-UPS AND CHILDREN

The play is set in the present [i.e., 1930/31] in Vienna and the Vienna Woods.

A piano score of the music used in the play is available from the holders of the performing rights: Thomas Sessler Verlag, A-1010 Vienna, Johannesgasse, Austria.

SCENE ONE

A quiet street in the Eighth District of Vienna.
From left to right: Oscar's prosperous butcher's shop with with sides of beef and veal, sausages, hams, and pigs' heads displayed in the window; next door is a doll hospital, "The Fairy King's Magic Cave," with jokes and tricks, skulls, dolls, toys, rockets, tin soldiers and a skeleton in its window; at the end of the row is a small tobacco shop with newspapers, magazines, and picture postcards outside the door. Over the doll hospital is a balcony with flowers belonging to the Fairy King's private apartment.

OSCAR (*in a white apron, standing in the doorway of his shop, manicuring his nails with a penknife. He occasionally cocks an ear toward the third floor where someone is playing Strauss's "Tales from the Vienna Woods" on an out-of-tune piano.*)
IDA (*a skinny, cute little eleven-year-old, comes out of the butcher's with her shopping bag and sets off to the right, stopping outside the doll hospital to look at the window display.*)
HAVLICHEK (*Oscar's assistant, a giant with blood-stained hands and apron, appears in the doorway, eating a small sausage. He is furious*) Stupid little bitch, stupid —
OSCAR Who?
HAVLICHEK (*pointing at Ida with his long knife*) That thing! That stupid little bitch had the cheek to say my blood sausage wasn't up to scratch . . . By Christ, I could slit her throat, I could, even if it meant she ran round with the knife sticking out of her neck like that pig yesterday. All the more fun, I say!
OSCAR (*smiling*) Really?
IDA (*sensing Oscar's eye on her, gets the creeps and suddenly runs off to the right*)
HAVLICHEK (*laughs*)
CAVALRY CAPTAIN (*enters from the left. He was pensioned off at the collapse of the Monarchy in 1918 and thus wears civilian clothes. He tips his hat to Oscar*)
OSCAR AND HAVLICHEK (*bow; the waltz ends*)

CAVALRY CAPTAIN I must say, that blood sausage yesterday — congratulations. First class!
OSCAR Tender, wasn't it?
CAVALRY CAPTAIN Melted in the mouth!
OSCAR Hear that, Havlichek?
CAVALRY CAPTAIN That man the one we have to thank?
HAVLICHEK Beg to report, Captain!
CAVALRY CAPTAIN Jolly good show!
HAVLICHEK You're a real gourmet, sir, a man of the world.
CAVALRY CAPTAIN (*to Oscar*) When I was on active service I was sent to all parts of the old Monarchy and I know quality when I see it.
OSCAR Tradition, Captain, tradition.
CAVALRY CAPTAIN If your poor dear mother were still alive she'd be proud of her son.
OSCAR (*smiling, flattered*) The Good Lord in his wisdom, Captain.
CAVALRY CAPTAIN Comes to all of us some day.
OSCAR A year ago today she was taken from us.
CAVALRY CAPTAIN Who?
OSCAR My Mama. It was after lunch, half past two, that she went to a better world.
(*silence*)
CAVALRY CAPTAIN Is it a year already?
(*silence*)
OSCAR You must excuse me, Captain, but I have to go and get dressed up in my Sunday best — for the Mass of the Dead. (*exit*)
CAVALRY CAPTAIN (*doesn't respond, his mind is elsewhere*)
(*silence*)
CAVALRY CAPTAIN Another year . . . until you're twenty they go at a walk, till forty at a trot, then it's a gallop . . .
(*silence*)
HAVLICHEK (*starts eating his sausage again*) It was a beautiful funeral, the old lady's.
CAVALRY CAPTAIN Yes, went off very well — (*turns his back on him and walks towards the tobacco shop; stops for a moment to look at the skeleton in the doll hospital; someone on the third floor*

is playing the piano again, the waltz "Over the Waves" by Juventino Rosas)
HAVLICHEK *(watches the Captain, spits out the sausage skin and goes back into the shop)*
MATHILDA *(in her fifties, tarted up, appears in the doorway of her tobacco shop)*
CAVALRY CAPTAIN *(doffs his hat)*
MATHILDA *(acknowledges his greeting)*
CAVALRY CAPTAIN Could I see the lottery draw —?
MATHILDA *(hands it to him from the stand by the door)*
CAVALRY CAPTAIN Much obliged, Madam. *(examines the list of winning numbers; the waltz suddenly breaks off in the middle of a bar)*
MATHILDA *(gloating)* Well, what have we won, Captain? The jackpot?
CAVALRY CAPTAIN *(giving the list back)* Never won anything at all, my dear lady. Devil knows why I buy the tickets. Most I've ever done is get my stake back.
MATHILDA You must be lucky in love, then.
CAVALRY CAPTAIN Was, was!
MATHILDA But Captain, with a profile like yours!
CAVALRY CAPTAIN Doesn't mean much, especially if you're a discriminating person — as I am. And that's an expensive characteristic to have. If the war had only lasted two more weeks I'd be drawing my major's pension now.
MATHILDA If the war had lasted two more weeks we'd have won.
CAVALRY CAPTAIN As far as anyone can judge —
(goes back into her shop)
MARIANNE *(comes out of the doll hospital with a customer — each time the shop door is opened chimes sound instead of a bell)*
CAVALRY CAPTAIN *(leafs though a newspaper, listening to them)*
THE LADY So I can rely on you?
MARIANNE Completely, Madam. We are the leading specialists in the district, and the oldest-established. The tin soldiers Madam requires will be there on time, that's guaranteed.
THE LADY Well, just to make sure there's no confusion: three boxes of seriously wounded and two of soldiers falling — includ-

ing cavalry, not just infantry. And I must have them by the day after tomorrow, in the morning, otherwise there'll be tears. It's my little boy's birthday on Friday and he's been dying to play at medical orderly for ages —

MARIANNE They'll be there, guaranteed, Madam. Thank you very much, Madam.

THE LADY Goodbye, then. (*exits left*)

FAIRY KING (*appears on the balcony in his dressing gown and mustache trainer*) Marianne! Are you there?

MARIANNE Papa?

FAIRY KING Where on earth are my garters?

MARIANNE The pink ones or the beige ones?

FAIRY KING I've only got the pink ones left!

MARIANNE In the cupboard, top left, at the back, on the right.

FAIRY KING Top left, at the back, on the right. Juvenal was right, the difficulty is *not* to write satire. (*exit*)

CAVALRY CAPTAIN (*to Marianne*) Busy as ever, Marianne, busy as ever?!

MARIANNE There's no disgrace in honest work, Captain.

CAVALRY CAPTAIN On the contrary. By the way, are congratulations in order yet?

FAIRY KING (*appears on the balcony again*) Marianne!

CAVALRY CAPTAIN Good morning, Fairy King.

FAIRY KING Good morning, Captain. Marianne, for the last time, where are my garters?

MARIANNE Where they always are.

FAIRY KING What kind of an answer is that, I ask you? The tone she takes. A slip of a girl! To her own father! Charming. My garters aren't where they always are.

MARIANNE Then they'll be in the chest of drawers.

FAIRY KING No.

MARIANNE In your bedside cabinet.

FAIRY KING No.

MARIANNE With your underpants.

FAIRY KING No.

MARIANNE Then I don't know where they are.

FAIRY KING I'm asking you for the very last time. Where are my garters?
MARIANNE I'm not a magician.
FAIRY KING (*shouting at her*) And I can't go the mass of the dead with my socks slipping down! Just because you don't look after my clothes properly! Get up here and find them! Avanti, avanti!
MARIANNE (*goes into the doll's hospital; the waltz "Over the Waves" is heard again*)
FAIRY KING (*listens*)
CAVALRY CAPTAIN Who's that playing?
FAIRY KING A girl on the third floor, she goes to the high school, a very talented child —
CAVALRY CAPTAIN A musical prodigy.
FAIRY KING An early developer — (*hums the tune, sniffs at the flowers, savoring their fragrance*)
CAVALRY CAPTAIN Spring is coming, Fairy King.
FAIRY KING And about time too! Even the weather's gone crazy.
CAVALRY CAPTAIN We all have.
FAIRY KING Not me.
(*silence*)
FAIRY KING We're in a sorry state, Captain, a sorry state. One can't even afford a maid nowadays. If it wasn't for my daughter —
OSCAR (*comes out of his shop, dressed in black with a top hat, pulling on a pair of black kid gloves*)
FAIRY KING I won't be a minute, Oscar. Dear little Marianne's done her vanishing trick with my garters again.
CAVALRY CAPTAIN Fairy King, allow me to offer you my own garters. I've taken to wearing elastic garters recently —
FAIRY KING Too kind. I appreciate the thought, but we must have order. Dear little Marianne will wave her magic wand and make them reappear.
CAVALRY CAPTAIN Our young bridegroom-to-be can congratulate himself on his good fortune.
OSCAR (*raises his hat and sketches a bow*)
FAIRY KING If God spares me.
CAVALRY CAPTAIN I wish you good day, gentlemen. (*exit; the waltz comes to an end*)

MARIANNE (*comes onto the balcony with the pink garters*) There, I've found your garters.
FAIRY KING See, I knew you would.
MARIANNE You put them in with the dirty washing by mistake — and I've just had to rummage through all the dirty clothes.
FAIRY KING Oh dear, how awful for you! (*gives her a fatherly smile and tweaks her cheek*) That's a good girl. Oscar's waiting outside. (*exit*)
OSCAR Marianne! Marianne!
MARIANNE Yes?
OSCAR Aren't you going to come down?
MARIANNE I have to anyway. (*exit*)
HAVLICHEK (*appears in the doorway of the butcher's, eating again*) Mr. Oscar, I meant to ask — say an Our Father in my name for your poor late mother, would you?
OSCAR Of course, Havlichek.
HAVLICHEK Thank you. (*exit*)
MARIANNE (*comes out of the doll hospital*)
OSCAR I'm so happy, Marianne. The year of mourning'll soon be over, I can take off the black armband tomorrow. Then on Sunday there'll be the official engagement and the wedding at Christmas. — Give us a kiss, Marianne, a little good-morning kiss.
MARIANNE (*gives him a kiss, but suddenly draws back*) Ouch! Why do you always have to bite?
OSCAR Did I do that just now?
MARIANNE Don't you know what you're doing?
OSCAR I could have sworn —
MARIANNE You always have to hurt me.
(*silence*)
OSCAR Angry?
(*silence*)
OSCAR Hey?
MARIANNE Sometimes I think you're longing for me to be a bad girl —
OSCAR Marianne! You know I'm a good Christian, you know I take the teachings of the Church seriously!

Tales from the Vienna Woods 63

MARIANNE Perhaps you think I don't believe in God? Shame on you!
OSCAR I didn't mean any disrespect! I know you despise me.
MARIANNE What a stupid thing to say, you idiot!
(*silence*)
OSCAR So you don't love me?
MARIANNE What is love?
(*silence*)
OSCAR Penny for them.
MARIANNE Oscar, if there's anything can separate us, it's you. Don't keep going on at me all the time, please —
OSCAR I'd like to be able to see inside your head, I'd like to strip off your skull and check up on what's going on inside —
MARIANNE But you can't do that.
OSCAR We're alone, and there's nothing we can do about it.
(*silence*)
OSCAR (*taking a box of chocolates out of his pocket*) Here's some chocolates, I'd almost forgotten them. Would you . . .? The ones in gold paper have liqueur . . .
MARIANNE (*mechanically pops a large chocolate in her mouth*)
FAIRY KING (*steps quickly out of the doll hospital; he too is dressed in black and has a top hat*) Here we are. What's that you've got there? Chocolates again? Very thoughtful of you, very thoughtful. (*tries one*) Pineapple! Splendid! (*to Marianne*) What about this fiancé of yours then, eh? Satisfied?
MARIANNE (*rushes off into the doll hospital*)
FAIRY KING (*bewildered*) What's got into her?
OSCAR One of her moods.
FAIRY KING A bit too full of herself. She doesn't know when she's well off!
OSCAR Come on Papa, we haven't much time — the mass —
FAIRY KING What a way to behave. I think you must be spoiling her. That's the last thing to do, my dear Oscar. You'll reap a bitter harvest. You can't imagine what I had to put up with in my marriage. And why? Not because my late wife was a cantankerous old bitch, God rest her soul, but because I was too considerate. Never lose your authority! Keep your distance! Patriarchy, not

matriarchy! Head up, thumbs down. Ave Caesar, morituri te salutant.

(*He exits with Oscar. The schoolgirl on the third floor is playing Ziehrer's waltz "On a Balmy Night."*)

MARIANNE (*appears in the shop window arranging things — she takes particular care with the skeleton*)

ALFRED (*enters from the left, sees Marianne from behind, stops and watches her*)

MARIANNE (*turns round, sees Alfred, is almost spellbound*)

ALFRED (*smiles*)

MARIANNE (*smiles too*)

ALFRED (*doffs his hat and bows in a charming manner*)

MARIANNE (*inclines her head in reply*)

ALFRED (*goes up to the window*)

MATHILDA (*appears in the door of her tobacconist's and watches Alfred*)

ALFRED (*drums on the windowpane with his fingers*)

MARIANNE (*suddenly gives him a horrified look and quickly lets the sunblind down — and the waltz breaks off in the middle of a bar again*)

ALFRED (*notices Mathilda*)

(*silence*)

MATHILDA Where are you off to?

ALFRED To see you, darling.

MATHILDA What's so interesting about the doll hospital, then?

ALFRED I was going to buy a doll for you.

MATHILDA And to think you throw your life away on a slob like that.

ALFRED I'm sorry.

(*silence*)

ALFRED (*chucks Mathilda under the chin*)

MATHILDA (*slaps him on the wrist*)

(*silence*)

ALFRED Who's the girl in there, then?

MATHILDA None of your goddam business.

ALFRED A pretty girl, very pretty even.

MATHILDA Ha-ha!

ALFRED A lovely figure. And I've never seen her before, must be Sod's law.
MATHILDA So what?
ALFRED Let's get this straight. I'm not going to take your hysterical fits of jealousy much longer! I refuse to let myself be pushed around! I don't have to put up with it!
MATHILDA Really?
ALFRED Don't go thinking I can't manage without your money.
(*silence*)
MATHILDA In that case perhaps it would be best —
ALFRED What?
MATHILDA Perhaps it would be best for both of us if we parted.
ALFRED But then for good! And amicably! And you must stick to it — There. That's what I owe you. Count it, please.
MATHILDA (*counts the money mechanically*)
ALFRED We lost nothing on the Saint-Cloud meeting and won on Le Tremblay. Outsiders. Hierlinger told me it was pure genius, what I was doing, I'm a real authority on the horses, he said.
(*silence*)
ALFRED You see? Everyone's got their good and their bad sides, it's quite normal. Let me whisper it in your ear: a true relationship between two human beings only really works when each one gets something out of the other. Anything else is fiddle-faddle. And on that understanding I don't think we should break up a relationship that mixes business with pleasure just because other people can get in the way of it. — What's that funny look you're giving me? (*shouts at her*) Take that look off your face, if you please.
(*silence*)
ALFRED And what do I do with your pension, Mrs. Chief-Clerk's Widow? Make it up to that of a deputy head of department, that's what I do with it! — What's wrong now?
MATHILDA I was just thinking of the grave.
ALFRED What grave?
MATHILDA His grave. Whenever I hear the word "chief clerk" I think of his grave.
(*silence*)

MATHILDA I don't look after his grave properly. Oh dear, it must be completely overgrown —
ALFRED Matty. If I have a win on the Maisons-Lafitte meeting tomorrow we'll have his grave properly tidied up. Fifty-fifty.)
MATHILDA (*suddenly kisses his hand*)
ALFRED No, don't do that. — (*takes the money off her again*) What's this? Crying?
MATHILDA (*in a tearful voice*) Not a bit of it. (*looks at herself in the mirror of her powder compact*) God, just look at me — high time I shaved myself again. (*puts on some lipstick, humming Chopin's funeral march*)

End of Scene One

SCENE TWO

The following Sunday in the Vienna Woods.
A clearing on the banks of the Blue Danube. The Fairy King, Marianne, Oscar, Mathilda, Alfred, a few distant relatives, among them Eric from Kassel in Prussia, and ugly little children dressed in white are on an outing together.
Now they form up into a picturesque group in order to be photographed by Oscar, who is still setting his tripod up; then he comes to his place next to Marianne and adopts a pose — he is working with a delayed-action shutter. After this has performed its function, the group starts to move.

FAIRY KING Just a moment! One more time! I think I must have wobbled.
OSCAR Oh, come on, Papa.
FAIRY KING You can't be too sure.
FIRST AUNT Oh yes.
SECOND AUNT It really would be a terrible shame.
FAIRY KING Come on then, one more time. *Da capo!*
OSCAR If we must. (*fiddles around with his camera again — again the delayed action works perfectly*)
FAIRY KING I thank you all.
GROUP (*gradually disintegrates*)
FIRST AUNT Oscar, I'd like to ask you a big favor — would you be a dear and take a picture of the children by themselves, they look so cute today —
OSCAR With the greatest of pleasure. (*poses the children and kisses the smallest girl*)
SECOND AUNT (*to Marianne*) Will you look at the way he groups them! Doesn't he just love them?! He obviously adores children, adores them! He'll make a perfect father. Touch wood! (*hugs Marianne and gives her a kiss*)
MATHILDA (*to Alfred*) Well that just about takes the Sachertorte!
ALFRED What Sachertorte?
MATHILDA You coming along with these people here when you know I'll be with them — after all that's happened between us.

ALFRED What's happened? We've gone our separate ways. And we agreed to stay good friends.
MATHILDA It's obvious you're not a woman — otherwise you'd show some respect for my feelings.
ALFRED What feelings? Still?
MATHILDA A woman can't forget just like that. There's something left inside me, in here, even if you are a lousy double-crosser.
ALFRED Oh, come on Matty, be reasonable.
MATHILDA (*suddenly spiteful*) That would suit you right down to the ground, wouldn't it?
(*silence*)
ALFRED Has the lousy double-crosser your permission to take his leave?
MATHILDA Who was it invited you to come?
ALFRED I'm not telling.
MATHILDA But it doesn't take a vivid imagination to guess.
ALFRED (*lights a cigarette*)
MATHILDA And where did we get acquainted? In the doll hospital?
ALFRED Shut your face.
FAIRY KING (*coming over to Alfred with Eric*) What's this I hear? You two haven't been introduced? Allow me: my nephew, Eric, the son of my sister-in-law's brother, by his second marriage, and — it's Zentner, isn't it?
ALFRED Yes.
FAIRY KING (*turning to Eric*) Mr. Zentner.
ERIC (*an ex-army bread-bag and water bottle dangling from his belt*) Pleased to meet you.
FAIRY KING Eric's a student. From Dessau.
ERIC From Kassel, uncle.
FAIRY KING Kassel or Dessau, I always mix them up. (*withdraws*)
ALFRED (*to Mathilda*) You two know each other?
MATHILDA Oh, we've known each other for ages.
ERIC We were introduced recently. We talked about the theater and what it says in the newspapers about the talkies being here to stay.

Tales from the Vienna Woods 69

ALFRED Fascinating! (*bows politely and withdraws; one of the Aunts plays "Your Tiny Hand Is Frozen" on her portable phonograph*)
ERIC (*listening*) *La Bohème*. Puccini — sublime!
MARIANNE (*now beside Alfred, listening*) Your tiny hand is frozen —
ALFRED That's *La Bohème*.
MARIANNE Puccini.
MATHILDA (*to Eric*) What operettas do you know?
ERIC They've got nothing to do with art!
MATHILDA How can you say a thing like that!
ERIC Do you know *The Brothers Karamazov*?
MATHILDA No.
ERIC That's art.
MARIANNE (*to Alfred*) There was a time when I wanted to study eurythmics and I dreamed of having my own institute, but my family has no understanding for that kind of thing. Papa always says women being financially independent of men is the last step on the road to Bolshevism.
ALFRED I know nothing about politics, but you can take it from me a man being financially dependent on a woman isn't a bundle of laughs either. It's a law of nature.
MARIANNE I don't believe it.
OSCAR (*is taking pictures of the Fairy King in various poses; the song on the portable phonograph has finished*)
ALFRED He likes taking pictures, does your fiancé.
MARIANNE He's mad about photography. We've known each other for eight years.
ALFRED And how old were you then? Oh, forgive me, that was just an automatic reaction.
MARIANNE Fourteen.
ALFRED Do forgive me.
MARIANNE He's a kind of childhood sweetheart. He's the boy next door, you see.
ALFRED And if he hadn't been the boy next door?
MARIANNE What do you mean?

ALFRED I mean it all comes down to the law of nature. And destiny.
(*silence*)
MARIANNE Destiny, yes. Actually, it's not what you think of when you say "love." On his side, perhaps, but otherwise — (*suddenly staring at Alfred*) What am I saying, I hardly know you — my God, you do have a way of drawing things out of a person —
ALFRED I don't want to draw anything out of you. On the contrary . . .
(*silence*)
MARIANNE Are you a hypnotist?
OSCAR (*to Alfred*) Excuse me. (*to Marianne*) Shall we go? (*holds out his arm for her to take and walks with her over to a picturesque clump of trees where the rest of the company is already sitting down to a picnic*)
ALFRED (*follows Oscar and Marianne and sits down with the others*)
FAIRY KING And what were we chatting about?
FIRST AUNT The transmigration of souls.
SECOND AUNT What on earth's the transmigration of souls?
ERIC It's Buddhist philosophy. Buddhists claim when a person dies their soul goes into an animal, into an elephant, for example.
FAIRY KING Crazy!
ERIC Or a snake.
FIRST AUNT Yuck!
ERIC Why yuck? That's just petty human prejudice. We should learn to appreciate the secret beauty of spiders, beetles, and millipedes —
SECOND AUNT (*interrupts him*) Don't be so revolting, please.
FIRST AUNT I'm feeling sick already.
FAIRY KING Nothing's going to spoil my appetite today. The creepy-crawly that could put me off my food just doesn't exist.
MATHILDA Now that's enough.
FAIRY KING (*rises and taps his glass with his knife*) Dear friends, by now it's an open secret that my dear daughter, Marianne, has looked favorably on my dear Oscar —
MATHILDA Good for her!

Tales from the Vienna Woods 71

FAIRY KING Quiet please, I won't be long — we are gathered here, that is, I have invited you here to celebrate an important juncture in the lives of two people in the bloom of youth, to celebrate it simply, but with dignity in a small but select group of family and friends. It saddens me to the heart that the Almighty in his wisdom did not see fit to allow my dear, departed wife, Marianne's loving mother, the joy of sharing this day with her only daughter. But I am sure that at this very moment she is up there on a star in eternity, looking down on us here. Now raise your glasses (*raises his glass*) to drink a heartfelt toast to the happy — and herewith officially engaged — couple, Oscar and Marianne. Three cheers for the happy couple, hip hip —
ALL Hooray.
FAIRY KING Hip hip —
ALL Hooray.
FAIRY KING Hip hip —
ALL Hooray.
IDA (*the cute, skinny little girl who criticized Havlichek's blood sausage in the first scene, in a white dress and holding a posy, steps forward and recites her poem, with a lisp, to the engaged couple*)
Oh love is like a sparkling jewel
Whose fires each day more brightly shine
And shall not fade while eyes reflect
The radiance of light divine.
ALL Well done! Bravo! God, isn't she cute!
IDA (*curtseys and gives the posy to Marianne*)
ALL (*in elated mood, smother Ida in caresses and congratulate the engaged couple; the portable phonograph plays the Wedding March and the Fairy King kisses Marianne on the forehead and Oscar on the lips; wiping the tears from his eyes, he lies down in his hammock*)
ERIC (*with his water bottle*) To Oscar and Marianne! Permit me to drink to you from this German Army water bottle. May you have health and happiness and many German children. Heil!
MATHILDA (*slightly tipsy*) And no niggers! Heil!

ERIC I'm sorry, madam, but that is not a matter for frivolity. It is something I hold sacred. You know my views on the racial problem.
MATHILDA A problematic young man, indeed — hey, don't go away, you complex character, you —
ERIC What do you mean, complex?
MATHILDA Interesting —
ERIC In what way?
MATHILDA D'you think I like the Jews? You're just a great big baby, aren't you — (*takes the great big baby's arm and drags him off; the grown-ups settle down among the trees and the children play games and keep disturbing them*)
OSCAR (*singing to his guitar*)
Joining hands in the hush of the night,
Our two hearts sing a song of delight.
In the spring we will both say, "I do,
I'll be true, true to you."
Soon the stork will be winging its way
With its bundle of joy, so they say.
Though our springtime is faded and gone,
In our children it still lives on.
(*plays the song once more, but doesn't sing, just hums; the others hum along with him, apart from Alfred and Marianne*)
ALFRED (*goes over to Marianne*) May I offer you my congratulations again?
MARIANNE (*closes her eyes*)
ALFRED (*places a lingering kiss on her hand*)
OSCAR (*observing what is going on, hands his guitar to the Second Aunt, sneaks over to where they are and suddenly pops up beside Marianne*)
ALFRED (*very formal*) Congratulations.
OSCAR Thank you.
ALFRED (*makes a very stiff bow and goes away*)
OSCAR (*watching him*) He's jealous because I've got you — the man's got no taste. Who is he anyway?
MARIANNE A customer.
OSCAR Known him a long time?

MARIANNE He came in yesterday and we got talking, not for long, then I gave him a call. He bought a party game.
MATHILDA (*in a shrill voice, waving a slip of paper*) Who is it, a he or a she? First tell me what their forfeit must be.
ERIC Go "moo" three times!
MATHILDA (*reads the name from the paper*) It's Aunt Hetty, Aunt Hetty.
FIRST AUNT (*goes down on all fours*) Moo, moo, moo.
(*laughter*)
MATHILDA Who is it, a he or a she? First tell me what their forfeit shall be.
FAIRY KING Go "baaa" three times.
MATHILDA It's you.
FAIRY KING Baa, baa, baa.
(*roars of laughter*)
MATHILDA Who is it, a he or a she? First tell my what their forfeit shall be.
SECOND AUNT Give us a demonstration.
ERIC What of?
SECOND AUNT Something they've learned.
MATHILDA Oscar! Did you hear, Oscar? You have to give us a demonstration.
ERIC Anything you like.
FAIRY KING Something you've learned.
(*silence*)
OSCAR Ladies and gentlemen, I'll give you a demonstration of something very useful. I've been studying the Japanese art of self-defense, what they call jujitsu. Pay attention now while I show you how easy it is to put your opponent out of action. (*suddenly falls on Marianne and demonstrates his holds on her*)
MARIANNE (*falls to the ground*) Ow! Ouch! Ouch!
FIRST AUNT That's too rough.
FAIRY KING Bravo! Bravo!
OSCAR (*to the First Aunt*) But that was only a demonstration hold. If it'd been for real I'd have broken her spine.
FIRST AUNT You wouldn't!

FAIRY KING (*giving Oscar a pat on the back*) Very neat! Beautifully done!
SECOND AUNT (*helping Marianne up*) And you such a delicate little thing! — Are there any more forfeits?
MATHILDA Sorry, they're all gone.
FAIRY KING Then I've got a suggestion to make. Let's all go for a swim. That water looks lovely and cool. I'm sweating like a monkey in a smokehouse.
ERIC Excellent idea.
MATHILDA But where is there for the women to change?
FAIRY KING Nothing simpler. Ladies on the right, gentlemen on the left. See you all in our Blue Danube.
(*Now the portable phonograph starts playing the "Blue Danube" waltz, and the women go off to the right, the men to the left; Mathilda and Alfred are the last to leave.*)
MATHILDA Alfred!
ALFRED What?
MATHILDA (*la-las the waltz tune and takes off her blouse*)
ALFRED And?
MATHILDA (*blows him a kiss*)
ALFRED Goodbye.
MATHILDA Just a minute. Is it the blushing bride my Lord fancies?
ALFRED (*stares at her, then quickly goes over and stands right in front of her*) Breathe on me.
MATHILDA Why should I do that?
ALFRED Breathe on me!
MATHILDA (*does so*)
ALFRED You alcoholic!
MATHILDA I'm just a little bit tiddly, that's all, you vegetarian. Man proposes, God disposes. It's not every day we celebrate an engagement — and a disengagement, you louse.
ALFRED Not that tone, if you please.
MATHILDA How can you stand there and not touch me, not touch me —
ALFRED Oh great! As if I ever touched you.
MATHILDA And on the seventeenth of March?
(*silence*)

ALFRED How you remember every little thing —
MATHILDA Everything. The good and the bad — (*suddenly holds her blouse in front of her*) Off you go. I want to get changed.
ALFRED As if I hadn't already seen —
MATHILDA (*shrieking*) Don't look at me like that! Off you go! Off you go!
ALFRED Hysterical old cow. (*goes off to the left.*)
MATHILDA (*alone, watches him leave*) Bastard. Swine. Shit. Beast. (*starts undressing*)
FAIRY KING (*appears from behind a bush in his swimming suit and watches her*)
MATHILDA (*in petticoat, panties and stockings; suddenly sees the Fairy King*) Jesus Mary and Joseph! You scoundrel, you! What are you, a voyeur?
FAIRY KING I'm not a pervert. Go on, don't let me stop you.
MATHILDA I can't. I'm embarrassed.
FAIRY KING What?! In these enlightened times?
MATHILDA I'm afraid I have this vivid imagination — (*trots off behind a bush*)
FAIRY KING (*sits down in front of the bush, sees Mathilda's corset, picks it up and sniffs at it*) Imagination or not, in these enlightened times the world's all gone to pot. No loyalty, no faith, no morals. Nothing's sure any more, everything's falling apart. Ripe for the Flood. (*puts the corset down; the scent isn't that overwhelming*) I'm just glad I've got Marianne provided for, a butcher's shop's still a sound business proposition —
MATHILDA'S VOICE And tobacconists?
FAIRY KING Them too! People'll always need to eat and smoke — but do conjuring tricks? Sometimes I get quite pessimistic when I start thinking about the future. I've not had it easy in my life, my late wife, for example — all that business with specialists —
MATHILDA (*appears in her bathing suit, still fiddling with the shoulder straps*) What did she die of, actually?
FAIRY KING (*staring at her breasts*) Her breast.
MATHILDA Oh, not cancer?
FAIRY KING Yes, cancer.
MATHILDA The poor thing.

FAIRY KING It wasn't much fun for me either. She had her left breast removed — she'd always been rather sickly, but her parents concealed it from me. — Now when I look at you, what a fine figure of a woman, truly majestic, yes, majestic.

MATHILDA (*starts to do some forward bends*) What do you men know of the tragedy that is woman? If we didn't spend all our time taking care of our appearance, dolling ourselves up —

FAIRY KING (*interrupts her*) Do you imagine I don't have to take care of my appearance?

MATHILDA Well you do, of course. But with men it's more the psychological things that count. (*starts showing off her calisthenics*)

FAIRY KING (*watches her, then does a few knee-bends*)

MATHILDA Phew, am I tired. (*throws herself down on the ground next to where he's standing*)

FAIRY KING The dying swan. (*sits down beside her*)

(*silence*)

MATHILDA May I lay my head in your lap?

FAIRY KING To the pure all things are pure.

MATHILDA (*lays her head in his lap*) The ground's still hard, you see — we had a long winter this year.

(*silence*)

MATHILDA (*softly*) Do you get the same feeling? When the sun shines on my skin I go all sort of —I don't know —

FAIRY KING You go all sort of? Go on, you can tell me.

(*silence*)

MATHILDA Just now you were playing with my corset, weren't you?

(*silence*)

FAIRY KING So what?

MATHILDA So what?

FAIRY KING (*suddenly throws himself over her and kisses her*)

MATHILDA God, such passion! I would never have thought it of you, you naughty boy.

FAIRY KING Am I very naughty?

MATHILDA Yes — Ooh, what are you doing!? — Just a minute, someone's coming. (*They quickly roll apart.*)

Tales from the Vienna Woods 77

ERIC (*in bathing trunks and carrying an air-rifle*) Excuse me, uncle, I'm sure you won't mind if I take the liberty of doing some shooting here?
FAIRY KING You want to what?
ERIC Do some shooting.
FAIRY KING You want to do some shooting here?
ERIC At the target on that beech tree over there. The day after tomorrow our Student Cadet Corps is having its shooting competition and so I'd like to take the liberty of getting a little practice in. I may, mayn't I?
MATHILDA Naturally!
FAIRY KING Naturally? (*to Mathilda, getting up*) Naturally! The Academic Cadet Corps! Very natural! You mustn't forget how to shoot. — I'm going to cool off. In our Blue Danube. (*aside*) You two can go jump in a lake!
ERIC (*loads, aims, and fires*)
MATHILDA (*watches; after the third shot*) I don't want to be a nuisance, but what are you studying?
ERIC Law. Second year. (*takes aim*) Company law. (*fires*)
MATHILDA Company law. Isn't that a bit boring?
ERIC (*loads*) When I graduate I've a good chance of finding a position as a legal adviser. (*takes aim*) In industry.
MATHILDA And how do you like it here in Vienna?
ERIC Magnificent baroque architecture!
MATHILDA And those sweet Viennese girls?
ERIC To be honest, young girls mean nothing to me. I was engaged once, but it was a big disappointment. Käthe was just too young to understand my essential nature. With young girls you're simply wasting your feelings. I prefer a more mature woman who can give you something in return. (*shoots*)
MATHILDA Where do you live?
ERIC I'd quite like to find some place else.
MATHILDA I've got a furnished room.
ERIC Cheap?
MATHILDA A giveaway.
ERIC That should suit me to a T.
MATHILDA Say, how about letting me have a go at shooting?

ERIC With pleasure.
MATHILDA The pleasure's all mine. (*taking the rifle from him*) You been in the army?
ERIC Unfortunately not, I was only born in 1911.
MATHILDA 1911 — (*takes a long time aiming*)
ERIC Halt! Attention! Fire!
MATHILDA (*doesn't fire; slowly lowers the rifle and looks at him with a serious expression on her face*)
ERIC What's wrong?
MATHILDA Ouch! (*doubles up and whimpers*) I've got these shooting pains —
(*silence*)
ERIC Can I do anything to help?
MATHILDA (*hands him back the rifle*) Take your rifle. Come on, let's get dressed. (*grabs his arm and goes off with him*)
ALFRED (*in beach robe and straw hat; passes them as they leave and doffs his hat in a sarcastic gesture.*
The sun has set; twilight; in the distance the portable phonograph is playing the Johann Strauss waltz "Voices of Spring")
MARIANNE (*emerges from the Blue Danube and sees Alfred*)
(*silence*)
ALFRED I knew you'd land here.
MARIANNE How did you know?
ALFRED I just knew.
(*silence*)
MARIANNE The Danube's as soft as velvet —
ALFRED As velvet.
MARIANNE Today I'd just like to take off. — Today you could sleep under the stars.
ALFRED No problem.
MARIANNE Isn't it terrible how civilized we are? Why can't we enjoy our natural impulses?
ALFRED What have we done to our natural impulses? Turned them into a straitjacket. No one's allowed to to act the way they want.
MARIANNE And no one wants to act the way they're allowed.
(*silence*)
ALFRED And no one's allowed to act they way they can.

MARIANNE And no one can act the way they ought —
ALFRED (*embraces her with a grand gesture and she does not resist in the least; a long kiss*)
MARIANNE (*in a breathy whisper*) I knew it, I knew it —
ALFRED So did I.
MARIANNE Do you really love me, the way you ought —?
ALFRED I have this instinct —
MARIANNE Me too — (*another long kiss*)
ALFRED Let's sit down. (*They sit down.*)
(*silence*)
MARIANNE I'm glad you're not stupid. I'm surrounded by stupid people. Even Papa's not very bright — and sometimes I even think he's trying to use me to get back at my late mother. She was very obstinate, you know.
ALFRED You think too much.
MARIANNE I feel fine now. I'd like to sing. I always feel like singing when I'm sad. (*hums and then stops*) Why aren't you saying anything?
Silence.
ALFRED Do you love me?
MARIANNE Very much.
ALFRED The way you ought to? I mean do you love me in a sensible way?
MARIANNE In a sensible way?
ALFRED I mean you won't do anything silly, will you? I couldn't accept responsibility if you did.
MARIANNE O Alfred, don't keep getting bogged down in dreary thoughts — look at the stars — they'll still be up there when we're under the ground —
ALFRED I'm going to be cremated.
MARIANNE Me too — Alfred, oh Alfred —
(*silence*)
MARIANNE Alfred — you struck me like lightning and you've taken hold of me — now I know for sure.
ALFRED What?
MARIANNE That I won't marry him —
ALFRED Marianne!

MARIANNE What's wrong?
ALFRED I haven't got any money.
MARIANNE Oh why must you talk about that now?
ALFRED Because it's my fundamental duty. Never in my life have I broken up an engagement, that's one of my cardinal principles. Fall in love, yes, but tear two people apart because of that — no, never! I haven't the moral right. It's a matter of principle!
(*silence*)
MARIANNE I wasn't wrong. You're someone special, someone with finer feelings. I feel doubly bound to you now. I'm not suited to Oscar, and that's that.
(*Meanwhile it has grown dark; rockets are let off nearby.*)
ALFRED Rockets. Celebrating your engagement.
MARIANNE Celebrating our engagement.
ALFRED They'll be looking for you.
MARIANNE Let them find us. Stay with me, Alfred, heaven sent you to me, my guardian angel —
(*Now there are Bengal lights, blue, green, yellow, red, and they light up Alfred and Marianne; and the Fairy King who is standing before them, his hand on his heart*)
MARIANNE (*gives a suppressed cry.*)
(*silence*)
ALFRED (*going up to the Fairy King*) Fairy King, sir —
FAIRY KING (*interrupts him*) Silence! I don't need any explanations, I heard everything. A scandal! At her engagement party! Lying around stark naked! I ask you! Marianne, get dressed! Let's just hope Oscar doesn't come along! Jesus, Mary and Jo-damn-sef!
ALFRED I'm quite prepared to take the consequences, if necessary.
FAIRY KING You're taking nothing! You're going to make yourself scarce, you — you —! This engagement is not going to fall through. Morality demands it — among other things. No one is to hear the slightest whisper, you scoundrel — on your word of honor.
ALFRED Word of honor.
MARIANNE No!!
FAIRY KING (*keeping his voice down*) Don't shout. Are you out of your mind? Get dressed, at the double — whore.

OSCAR (*appears and sizes up the situation*) Marianne! Marianne!
FAIRY KING That's torn it.
(*silence*)
ALFRED Your fiancée's been swimming. She's just got out of the water.
MARIANNE Don't lie. Don't lie like that. I haven't been swimming and I've had enough. I've had enough of being pushed around by the lot of you. The slave has broken her fetters — there (*throws her engagement ring in Oscar's face*) I'm not going to let you foul up my life. It's my life. At the last minute God has sent this man to me. — No, I'm not going to marry you, I'm not going to marry you, I'm not going to marry you! Our doll hospital can go to pot for all I care, and the sooner the better.
FAIRY KING My only child! I won't forget this!
(*Silence; while Marianne is shouting the rest of the party come along to listen, with expressions of interest and glee on their faces.*)
OSCAR (*going up to Marianne*) Marianne, I just hope you never have to go through what I'm going through now. — I'll go on loving you, you can't escape me — and thank you for everything.
(*exit*)
(*silence*)
FAIRY KING What are you anyway?
ALFRED Me?
MATHILDA He's nothing, nothing!
FAIRY KING A nothing to boot! I haven't got a daughter anymore.
(*goes off with the others; Alfred and Marianne are left alone; the moon is shining*)
ALFRED Please forgive me.
MARIANNE (*gives him her hand*)
ALFRED For not wanting to marry you — it was my sense of responsibility that was responsible for that. I'm not worthy of your love, I can't support you, I'm nothing, a nobody —
MARIANNE I can take anything now. Let me make something, somebody out of you. With you I seem to grow, to expand —
ALFRED And you raise me up to your level. Before you I feel so small, spiritually —

MARIANNE And I'm leaving myself behind, I can see myself disappearing — can't you see it too, I'm a long way away from myself already — there I am, down there, I can hardly see myself anymore — I want to have a child by you.

End of Scene Two

SCENE THREE

In St. Stephen's Cathedral
A congenital idiot is kneeling at the side altar to St. Anthony.
Marianne is kneeling three rows behind him.
Alfred enters quietly.
From one of the altars comes the jingle of bells that accompanies the consecration; Marianne and the Idiot bow their heads reverently.
Silence.

ALFRED (*softly*) Is it going to go on much longer?
MARIANNE If it's too long for you then leave me alone.
ALFRED You won't have to tell me that twice.
MARIANNE Then go!
ALFRED I suppose I can't go quickly enough for you?
MARIANNE Not so loud, we're not at home.
IDIOT (*turns round and stares at the two of them, then goes back to his rosary*)
ALFRED (*kneels down beside Marianne; with a nasty grin*) My Maid of Orleans.
MARIANNE Please, let me get on with my prayers.
ALFRED What's the point of this new sport? Don't you feel happy with yourself.
MARIANNE Do you maybe?
(*silence*)
ALFRED Even your St. Anthony of Padua won't get me a job, just remember that, young lady. I'd like to meet the saint who would help an ordinary mortal earn anything, even a few coppers. — Hold it! (*grabs Marianne by the arm as she tries to get up, and forces her back onto her knees*)
MARIANNE Ouch!
IDIOT (*watches the pair of them again, and keeps on doing so for the rest of the scene*)
ALFRED And who was it made me give up the horses? It's a whole year since I last spoke to a bookie, never mind a good tipster. There's no point in going back to it now — a new season, new

favorites, two-year-olds, three-year-olds — I'm completely out of touch with the new generation of horses. And why? Because instead of betting on the immoral totalizer I'm trying to sell a moral skin creme which no one's buying because it's useless.
MARIANNE People just haven't any money.
ALFRED Oh yes, we must stand up for the people.
MARIANNE I'm not blaming you, it's not your fault.
ALFRED I should hope not.
MARIANNE As if I could do anything about the economic crisis.
ALFRED There you go again. Who was it gave me the ridiculous advice to wear out my shoe leather as a cosmetics salesman? You! (*stands up*)
(*silence*)
MARIANNE Once you told me I raised you up, spiritually —
ALFRED I never said that. I can't have said that. And if I did, I was mistaken.
MARIANNE (*shoots up off her knees, horrified*) Alfred!
ALFRED Not so loud. We're not at home.
MARIANNE Alfred, I'm so frightened —
ALFRED You're seeing ghosts.
MARIANNE If you've forgotten everything, Alfred —
IDIOT (*puts on a malicious grin*)
ALFRED (*pointing to the idiot*) Just look at the stupid moron —
MARIANNE Leave the poor thing alone. (*quietly cries to herself*)
(*silence*)
ALFRED As far as I'm concerned, I don't believe in life after death, but of course I do believe in some higher being, he must exist, otherwise we wouldn't. (*strokes her hat*) Calm down now, people are looking.
(*silence*)
MARIANNE (*with a wide-eyed stare*) When I was a little girl and I'd lost something, I only had to say, "St. Anthony, please help me," and I found it straight away.
ALFRED Goodbye, then.
MARIANNE You'll come to meet me?
ALFRED Of course. Bien sure. (*exit*)

MARIANNE (*watches him leave; she gradually becomes aware of a confessional, the contours of which slowly emerge from the darkness; she goes over to it hesitantly* — *bells ring and people from the congregation walk past her, little first communicants and old cripples* — *a server douses all the candles on the altar to St. Anthony and now all that can be seen is the confessional with Marianne kneeling in it, everything else has merged into the darkness; the Idiot has gone and the bells stopped ringing; the whole world is very quiet.*)
FATHER CONFESSOR (*looks like Oscar Wilde*) Let us just go through it again: you have been disobedient and ungrateful, and brought deep sorrow, anguish, and distress on your poor, aged father, who loves you above all else and has always had your best interests at heart — you abandoned your fiancé, a decent, God-fearing man, for a depraved good-for-nothing, to satisfy your own fleshly lusts —silence! We know all about that! And now you have been living with that miserable wretch for more than a year without the holy sacrament of marriage, and in this terrible state of mortal sin you conceived and bore your child — when?
MARIANNE Two months ago.
FATHER CONFESSOR And you have not even thought fit to have this child of sin and shame baptized. Now you tell me: can any good come of all this? No, never! But that's not all. You even went so far as to try to kill it in your womb.
MARIANNE No, that was him! I only submitted to it for his sake!
FATHER CONFESSOR Only for his sake?
MARIANNE He didn't want any children because things are getting worse and worse in the world, and will for the foreseeable future — but I — no, every time he looks at me it pierces me to the heart that I tried to get rid of him before he was born.
(*silence*)
FATHER CONFESSOR Are you looking after the child?
MARIANNE No.
FATHER CONFESSOR Where is it, then?
MARIANNE Boarded out with a family.
FATHER CONFESSOR Are they God-fearing folk?
MARIANNE Definitely.

(*silence*)
FATHER CONFESSOR So you repent your sin in trying to kill it?
MARIANNE Yes.
FATHER CONFESSOR And in living with that good-for-nothing animal without the blessing of the Church?
(*silence*)
MARIANNE I once thought I had found the man who would be everything to me. —
FATHER CONFESSOR Do you repent?
(*silence*)
MARIANNE Yes.
FATHER CONFESSOR And that you conceived and bore your child in a state of mortal sin, do you repent that?
(*silence*)
MARIANNE No. That's impossible —
FATHER CONFESSOR What is that you're saying?
MARIANNE He's still my child —
FATHER CONFESSOR But you —
MARIANNE (*interrupts him*) No, I can't do that. In fact I get afraid I might regret having had him. No, I'm happy that I have him, very happy —
(*silence*)
FATHER CONFESSOR If you cannot bring yourself to repent it, what do you want from the Lord God?
MARIANNE I thought the Lord God might say a word to me —
FATHER CONFESSOR You only come to him when things are bad, then?
MARIANNE When things are fine I know He's with me — but, no, I can't believe He would want me to repent that — that would be against all natural feeling —
FATHER CONFESSOR Go then. And do not come to the Lord again until you have cleared your soul of this sin. (*makes the sign of the cross*)
MARIANNE In that case I'm sorry — (*leaves the confessional, which merges back into the darkness; now the murmur of a litany can be heard, the voices of the priest and the congregation*

gradually becoming more and more distinct; Marianne listens, the litany ends with the Lord's Prayer; Marianne's lips move.)
(*silence*)
MARIANNE Amen —
(*silence*)
MARIANNE If there is a God — what do you have in store for me, Lord? O merciful Lord, I was born in Vienna, in the Eighth District, and I went to junior high there. I'm not a bad woman — do you hear me? — What do you have in store for me, merciful Lord?

End of Scene Three

SCENE FOUR

Back in the quiet street in the Eighth District, outside Oscar's butcher's shop, the doll hospital, and Mathilda's tobacco store. The sun is shining, just as in the good old days, and the schoolgirl on the second floor is still playing Strauss's "Tales from the Vienna Woods."

HAVLICHEK (*standing in the doorway of the shop, stuffing himself with a sausage*)
EMMA (*a maid of all work, is standing beside Havlichek, holding her shopping bag; she is listening to the music*) Mr. Havlichek —
HAVLICHEK I'm sorry?
EMMA Music is lovely, isn't it?
HAVLICHEK I think I could imagine something even more lovely, Miss Emma.
EMMA (*hums along with the waltz*)
HAVLICHEK It would all depend on you, Miss Emma.
EMMA Seems to me you're a real Casanova, Mr. Havlichek.
HAVLICHEK Call me Ladislaus.
(*pause*)
EMMA Last night I dreamed of your boss.
HAVLICHEK Couldn't you think of anything better to dream of?
EMMA Mr. Oscar always has those big, melancholy eyes. You feel really sorry for him whenever he looks at you.
HAVLICHEK It's love that's done it.
EMMA What do you mean by that?
HAVLICHEK I mean that he's in love with a worthless woman and she dumped him — it's eighteen months ago now — and ran off with this other worthless guy.
EMMA And he still loves her? I think that's really lovely.
HAVLICHEK I think it's dumb.
EMMA But a grand passion like that is so romantic —
HAVLICHEK No, it's unhealthy! Just look at the way he looks, he's tormenting himself all the time — he doesn't even notice any other women, and he's got all that money and he's well known round here, there's any number of rich young girls just waiting for him to

ask, but no, he has to set his mind on that horny bitch. — Devil only knows what he gets up to.
EMMA And what do you mean by that?
HAVLICHEK I mean that no one knows where he goes to shoot his load.
EMMA Oh, you are terrible, you know!
(*pause*)
HAVLICHEK Emma, tomorrow's a holiday and I'll be at the terminus of the seventy-eight.
EMMA But I can't manage before three.
HAVLICHEK No problem there.
(*pause*)
EMMA Half past three, then — and don't forget what you promised, Ladislaus, that you'll be a good boy and behave yourself — (*exit*)
HAVLICHEK (*watches her go and spits out the sausage skin*) Stupid little bitch, stupid —
OSCAR (*comes out of the shop*) Don't forget we've got that pig to slaughter. You'll have to cut its throat, I'm not in the mood today.
(*pause*)
HAVLICHEK Can I be frank with you, Mr. Oscar?
OSCAR Is it about the pig?
HAVLICHEK It's about a pig all right, but not the same one. — Mr. Oscar, you shouldn't take it to heart so, all that business with your ex-fiancée, women are two-a-penny. Any cripple can get a woman, even men with the clap. And when you get down to the important things, they're all the same, women, believe me, I'm telling you the way things are. Women are all body and no soul. That's why you shouldn't treat them gently, that's a mistake, you have to let them feel the sharp side of your tongue right away.
(*pause*)
OSCAR Woman is a mystery, Havlichek. A sphinx. I once showed Marianne's handwriting to different graphologists. The first said that's the handwriting of a vampire, the second, that's a girl you can be good friends with, the third, that's the ideal housewife, an angel.
CAVALRY CAPTAIN (*enters from the left and tips his hat to Oscar*)

OSCAR AND HAVLICHEK (*bow*)
CAVALRY CAPTAIN I must say, that blood sausage yesterday — congratulations. First class!
HAVLICHEK Tender, wasn't it?
CAVALRY CAPTAIN Melted in the mouth. (*goes over to the tobacco store*)
HAVLICHEK (*goes into the shop*)
MATHILDA (*appears in the doorway of her tobacco store*)
CAVALRY CAPTAIN (*doffs his hat*)
MATHILDA (*acknowledges his greeting*)
CAVALRY CAPTAIN Could I see the lottery draw?
MATHILDA (*hands it to him from the stand by the door*)
CAVALRY CAPTAIN Much obliged, madam. (*examines the list of winning numbers; the waltz finishes*)
ERIC (*comes out of the tobacco store, tips his hat to Mathilda and is about to leave*)
MATHILDA Just a minute, what's that you've got there?
ERIC Five *Memphis*.
MATHILDA What, again? Smoking just like a grown-up!
CAVALRY CAPTAIN AND OSCAR (*prick up their ears*)
ERIC (*keeping his voice down*) If I don't smoke, I can't work. If I don't work I'll never get my traineeship, and if I don't manage that I'm hardly likely ever be in a position to pay you back what I owe you.
MATHILDA What do you mean, what you owe me?
ERIC You know very well what I mean! I'm a man of my word.
MATHILDA Are you trying to make me cry again?
ERIC It's a matter of honor. I pay my debts, right down to the very last pfennig, even if the repayments last a hundred years. No one can say anything against us. It's a matter of honor! And now I've got a lecture to go to. (*exit*)
MATHILDA (*stares at him as he goes*) Swine! Crook! A matter of honor! Beast!
CAVALRY CAPTAIN AND OSCAR (*grin to themselves*)
FAIRY KING (*sees The Lady to the door of the doll hospital*)
THE LADY I bought some tin soldiers from here before — but then I was served by a very polite young girl.

FAIRY KING (*in a surly tone*) Could be.
THE LADY Your daughter?
FAIRY KING No!
THE LADY Pity. So you won't order me another box of tin soldiers?
FAIRY KING I told you in the shop, all these special orders cause much too much paperwork — and just for one box. Why don't you buy your darling boy something similar? A top-quality trumpet, perhaps?
THE LADY No! Goodbye. (*turns on her heel in irritation and leaves*)
FAIRY KING Your servant madam. — Drop dead! (*goes over to Oscar and talks to him*)
CAVALRY CAPTAIN (*to Mathilda; in a malicious tone*) And how are we today, madame?
MATHILDA (*getting her own back*) And what have we won today, Captain?
CAVALRY CAPTAIN (*handing back the list*) It's a crying shame, isn't it? Or do you think it's right, the way His Majesty the Fairy King is treating Marianne? I just don't understand it. If I were a grandfather — and anyway, it's so easy to slip off the straight and narrow — but to let her go to rack and ruin like that —
MATHILDA Do you know any details?
CAVALRY CAPTAIN I once had a colonel's wife, that is, the whole regiment had her — oh, what am I saying!? She was the wife of our colonel, and he had an illegitimate child with a show girl, but his wife took it into her house as if it were her own flesh and blood, because she couldn't have children herself. When you look at the attitude of his majesty over there — no comparison.
MATHILDA I don't understand. What has your colonel's wife to do with Marianne?
CAVALRY CAPTAIN No one understands anyone else any more. Sometimes we don't even understand ourselves. I tell you, if we hadn't lost the war —
MATHILDA Where is Marianne living?
CAVALRY CAPTAIN (*with a cryptic smile*) That will all be announced publicly — at the appropriate moment. I wish you good day. (*exit*)

FAIRY KING (*to Oscar*) Yes, yes, I agree the European countries must get together — if there's another war we'll all be destroyed — but does that mean we have to put up with anything? Look at the liberties those Czechs are taking again! I'm telling you, any day now there's going to be another war. Has to be! There'll always be wars.
OSCAR That may well be. But it would mean the end of civilization as we know it.
FAIRY KING Civilization? What civilization? War's a law of nature. Just like competition in business. As it happens, my business has no competition because it's a specialist store and still it's going downhill. I can't run it on my own any longer, I start twitching whenever a customer comes in. — In the old days there was my wife, and when she started getting poorly, Marianne was big enough already —
OSCAR How big?
FAIRY KING That big.
(*silence*)
OSCAR If I were a grandfather —
FAIRY KING (*interrupts him*) I am not a grandfather, I'll have you know.
OSCAR Sorry.
(*silence*)
FAIRY KING By the way, I meant to ask you. You're slaughtering a pig today, aren't you?
OSCAR That is my intention.
FAIRY KING You'll keep back a nice bit of kidney for me, won't you?
OSCAR Of course.
FAIRY KING I wish you good day, then. (*goes back into the doll hospital; the schoolgirl on the second floor is playing the piano again, the waltz "Over the Waves."*)
ALFRED (*enters slowly from the left*)
OSCAR (*is about to go back into the shop when he sees Alfred, who doesn't notice him; Oscar secretly observes Alfred.*)

ALFRED (*stops outside the doll hospital, puts on a "happy memories" act, then stops in the doorway to the tobacco store and stares in.*)
(*pause*)
ALFRED (*raises his hat*)
(*pause*)
MATHILDA (*had gone back into the store while Oscar and the Fairy King were talking; now she comes out slowly — and the waltz breaks off again, in the middle of a bar again*)
ALFRED Could I have five *Memphis*?
MATHILDA No.
(*silence*)
ALFRED I thought this was a tobacco store.
MATHILDA You thought wrong, then.
(*silence*)
ALFRED I just happened to be passing, by chance —
MATHILDA Aha.
ALFRED Yes.
(*silence*)
MATHILDA And how are we today?
ALFRED Not too bad.
MATHILDA Aha. And your lovely fiancée?
ALFRED That's all over. Since July.
MATHILDA Aha.
(*silence*)
ALFRED Everything OK?
MATHILDA All my needs are catered for.
ALFRED All?
MATHILDA All. He's a law student.
ALFRED And that's the kind of person who gets to be a judge!
MATHILDA Sorry?
ALFRED Congratulations.
MATHILDA Where's your fiancée living, then?
ALFRED No idea.
MATHILDA And the little boy?
ALFRED I've completely lost touch with both of them.
(*silence*)

MATHILDA You really are a grade one bastard, even your greatest enemy would have to give you that.
ALFRED Mathilda. Let the one among you who is without sin cast the first stone at me.
MATHILDA Are you ill?
ALFRED No. Just tired. Harassed. I'm not as young as I was.
MATHILDA Since when?
ALFRED I've just spent four weeks in France. In Nancy. I thought I might find something more suitable for me there in my original profession. Originally I was a waiter and here I'd have to start right back at the bottom again.
MATHILDA And how are the horses?
ALFRED I'm out of practice. And I'm short of capital —
MATHILDA And the women in France?
ALFRED Just the same as everywhere. Ungrateful.
(*silence*)
MATHILDA When I've got some spare time I'll feel sorry for you.
ALFRED You'd like me to be in a bad way?
MATHILDA Is everything coming up roses, then?
ALFRED Is that what you'd like to hear?
(*silence*)
ALFRED I just happened to be passing. By chance — but I know when I'm not wanted (*exit — and now the girl on the second floor takes up the waltz "Over the Waves" again*)
MATHILDA (*goes over to Oscar*) Guess who I've just been talking to?
OSCAR I saw him.
MATHILDA You did? He's in a bad way.
OSCAR I heard everything.
(*pause*)
MATHILDA He's still as proud as Lucifer, the swine —
OSCAR Pride comes before a fall. — Poor Marianne —
MATHILDA I do believe you're capable of going and marrying Marianne, now that she's free again.
OSCAR If she didn't have that child . . .
MATHILDA If anyone had done that to me —
OSCAR I still love her — perhaps the child'll die —

MATHILDA You mustn't say that!
OSCAR Who knows? The mills of God grind slow, but they grind exceeding small. I'm happy to take any suffering upon myself, for whom the Lord loveth he correcteth.   And chasteneth. And scourgeth. On red-hot coals, in boiling lead —
MATHILDA (*screams at him*) Stop it, please stop it!
OSCAR (*smiles*)
HAVLICHEK (*comes out of the butcher's*) So what do you want me to do? Shall I slaughter this pig or not?
OSCAR No, Havlichek. I'll do it myself, I'll slaughter the pig —

End of Scene Four

SCENE FIVE

At a wine garden outside Vienna. A small band with guitars and accordion is playing dance music and popular songs. Petals from the fuit-treees in blossom rain down. The whole place is buzzing and everyone is slightly high on the wine, including the Fairy King, Mathilda, and Eric.

Out there where green the wine grows
And blue the Danube flows,
A cottage peeps through the vines
There lives a maid of mine,
With lips as red as blood —
Her kisses taste so good —
And eyes a violet hue,
Beside the Danube so blue.

There'll be new wine each year
When we are gone from here,
There'll be pretty girls to kiss
And we will not be missed.
(*For a moment there is a deathly hush in the wine garden — then everyone starts singing again, three times louder than before.*)
So let's all go to Nussdorf soon,
We'll have a lot of fun,
The evening's just begun,
We'll dance and sing a merry tune
And then roll home and sleep
Till the afternoon, till the afternoon.
(*Enthusiastic applause; people are dancing between the tables; everyone is pretty fuddled by now.*)

FAIRY KING Bravo! Bravissimo! I'm my old self again tonight! Encore! Da capo! (*As a couple dance past he grabs the girl's breasts.*)
HER PARTNER (*slaps his hand*) Hands off her boobs.
THE GIRL They're my boobs, if you please.

ERIC Uncle Fairy King, in honor of this most excellent Viennese wine tavern and, last but not least, of your good self, allow me to take the liberty of raising the Salamander, a special fraternity toast — Hail! Hail! Hail! (*tries to push his glass round and round then drum with it on the table, but only succeeds in spilling most of his wine*)
MATHILDA Hey, hey, take it easy, young man. Just look at that, he's spilled it all over me.
ERIC More wine! Waiter, more wine! The Salamander must rise, the fraternity's honor's at stake. Waiter!
FAIRY KING Did he soak you? You poor thing.
MATHILDA Through and through. To the skin.
FAIRY KING What, right through to your skin —
MATHILDA Are you off your head too?
ERIC The honor of the fraternity is at stake! Old Prussia's not dead yet! Attention! (*gets up, crashes his heels together and stands at attention, absolutely still*)
FAIRY KING What's the matter with him?
MATHILDA I'm used to it by now. When he's had one too many he gives orders to himself.
FAIRY KING I don't know how he can keep still for so long. A smart lad, sturdy too. You have to admire him. Things are looking up. (*falls under the table*)
MATHILDA Jesus and Mary!
FAIRY KING The chair broke. Waiter! Another chair! Hey, another chair! (*sings along with the music*) "Just an innocent kiss on the shoulder, I said — and I felt the full force of her fan round my head —"
WAITER (*brings a gigantic helping of salami*)
MATHILDA Salami, Eric. Salami!
ERIC Battalion — at ease! Form a line to collect field rations! At the double! (*grabs the food with his hand and stuffs it down at incredible speed*)
FAIRY KING What an appetite!
MATHILDA Get that down you.
FAIRY KING Don't be so greedy!
MATHILDA He's not paying!

FAIRY KING And he he's not singing for it either.
(*pause*)
MATHILDA (*to Eric*) Yes, why don't you sing?
ERIC (*his mouth full*) Because I suffer from chronic catarrh.
MATHILDA You smoke too much.
ERIC (*bellows at her*) Don't start that again!
CAVALRY CAPTAIN (*appears at their table in a paper hat and high spirits*) The lovely Mathilda. What a pleasant surprise! Your servant, my dear. Good evening to you, Fairy King.
FAIRY KING Cheers, Captain! You'll have to excuse me a minute, where's the men's room?
CAVALRY CAPTAIN Right over there, beside the bar. (*The Fairy King heads for the toilet.*)
MATHILDA Can I offer you some of my salami, Captain? (*Eric chokes on his sausage and fixes a baleful stare on the Captain.*)
CAVALRY CAPTAIN Too kind, dear lady. No, no, really, I couldn't, (*pops two thick slices into his mouth*) I've had two dinners already. I'm with that party over there and I've got a visitor, a schoolfriend of my brother — he disappeared in Siberia during the war, you know — an American.
MATHILDA Oh, from the land of the free!
CAVALRY CAPTAIN But born in Vienna. He's been over there in the States for twenty years now and it's his first time back in Europe. There were tears in his eyes when we drove through the Hofburg this morning. — He's a self-made man. Out there a man has to do things himself.
MATHILDA Oh, you naughty boy!
CAVALRY CAPTAIN Yes. And now I'm showing him round his hometown — we started yesterday — it's been one long spree since then.
MATHILDA Still waters run deep.
CAVALRY CAPTAIN And not only in America.
ERIC (*in caustic tone*) Is that so?
(*pause*)
MATHILDA Do you gentlemen know each other?
CAVALRY CAPTAIN By sight —
ERIC You're Austrian? Fine uniforms and faint hearts.

MATHILDA Eric!
CAVALRY CAPTAIN What did he say?
ERIC I said that in the war the Austrians hadn't the stomach for a real fight, and if it hadn't been for us Prussians —
CAVALRY CAPTAIN (*interrupts him*) — there wouldn't have been a war at all.
ERIC And Sarajevo? Bosnia-Herzegovina?
CAVALRY CAPTAIN What do you know about the World War, you little know-all? What you learned at school, that's all.
ERIC At least that's better than teaching old Jewesses to play bridge!
MATHILDA Eric!
CAVALRY CAPTAIN Well at least that's better than being kept by old women who own tobacco stores!
MATHILDA Captain!
CAVALRY CAPTAIN I'm terribly sorry. That was a *faux pas*. A slip of the tongue. (*kisses her hand*) Most unfortunate, but that young whippersnapper over there has never earned a penny of his own in all his life.
ERIC (*stands up*) Sir!
MATHILDA No duel, for God's sake!
ERIC I could demand satisfaction.
CAVALRY CAPTAIN Would you like to take it to the honor court?
MATHILDA Quiet! People are looking.
ERIC I'm not just going to stand here to be insulted.
CAVALRY CAPTAIN It's impossible to insult you.
MATHILDA But gentlemen, gentlemen! When everyone's enjoying themselves!
CAVALRY CAPTAIN I refuse to accept comments like that from this Prussian. Where were your Hohenzollerns when our Habsburgs ruled the Holy Roman Empire? Out in the backwoods!
ERIC That does it!
CAVALRY CAPTAIN There's twenty groschen, go and get your crest clipped, you cockatoo.
THE AMERICAN (*comes over; drunk*) Oh my friend, my very best friend — What's this? Company? Friends? Do introduce me, please — my dear, dear friend — (*embraces the Captain*)

ERIC I'm off —

MATHILDA You sit down. If you can eat my salami, then at least you can try to be nice to me — and keep your face shut, or you'll feel the back of my hand —

CAVALRY CAPTAIN Where's our Fairy King? He hasn't fallen down the can, has he?

FAIRY KING (*appears*) Here I am. It was a pretty tight squeeze in there, I can tell you! Who's this?

CAVALRY CAPTAIN A dear friend of mine from America.

THE AMERICAN America! New York! Chicago and Sing Sing! That's me on the outside, but inside there's still a good, old, honest Viennese heart of gold beating, Vienna, city of my dreams — and the Wachau, where green the wine grows — and the castles along the Blue Danube (*sings along with the music*) Danube so blue, so blue, so blue —

ALL (*hum along and sway in time to the music*)

THE AMERICAN Ladies and gentlemen. Many things have changed in recent times, storms and hurricanes have swept over the face of the earth, earthquakes and tornadoes, and I had to start right at the bottom, but this is where I belong, this is where I feel right, this is where I like to be, and this is where I'd like to die. God's an Austrian and He lives in Mariazell!

Sings.

My mother was a Vienna girl, she loved Vienna so,
And at my mother's breast, I learned to love best
My Vienna, my true heart of gold.

ALL (*apart from Eric of course, sing*)

Vienna, my one, my own,
My longing heart dreams of you alone.
In all the beautiful cities I've seen
I yearn for you, my Wien.

THE AMERICAN Long live Vienna! Home! And those beautiful Viennese women! Vienna for the Viennese! Long live the Viennese — all of us! Hip hip —

ALL (*except Eric*) Hooray! Hooray!

(*Everyone drinks to everyone.*)

MATHILDA Come on Eric, drink up!

ERIC No. It's a matter of honor.
MATHILDA Shall I order more salami?
ERIC That remark, madam, is typical of your crude outlook on life.
MATHILDA Stay!
ERIC Attention! Platoon — about face!
MATHILDA Halt!
ERIC Platoon — by the right flank — quick march! (*exit*)
MATHILDA Platoon — resume position! Resume position!
FAIRY KING Let the drunken brat go. Do I have some relations!
MATHILDA I'll let him go for good — I can see it coming, I can really —
FAIRY KING With the fine figure you've got — I should have married you, with you I'd have had a quite different daughter —
MATHILDA Don't keep harping on about Irene. I never could stand her.
THE AMERICAN Who's Irene?
FAIRY KING She was my wife.
THE AMERICAN Oh, sorry!
FAIRY KING Nothing to be sorry about. — and why shouldn't I bitch about Irene? Just because she's dead? She ruined my whole life!
MATHILDA There's something demonic about you.
FAIRY KING (*sings*)
Now my old woman's dead,
That's why I'm feeling sad.
I think I'll never find
Another of her kind.
No one can know
How the teardrops flow.
She was my all, I miss her so. Hey!
THE AMERICAN (*comes to with a start*) Hey! If I'm not mistaken, it's beginning to rain. But we won't let that bother us. We won't go home till the morning — even if it starts raining bullfrogs. We won't put up with it! (*shakes his finger at the heavens*) Our Father who art raining in Heaven. Come on everyone, off we go, the drinks are on me!
ALL Hooray!

THE AMERICAN Off we go, then. Follow me. Forward march.
MATHILDA Where to?
THE AMERICAN Anywhere we'll have a ceiling over our heads. Anywhere out of the rain. The Moulin Bleu!
(*loud applause*)
CAVALRY CAPTAIN Wait a minute! Not the Moulin Bleu, friends. If it's going to be a night club let's make it Maxim's.
(*For a moment there is a deathly hush.*)
FAIRY KING Why Maxim's.
CAVALRY CAPTAIN Because there's something special at Maxim's.
FAIRY KING What kind of thing?
CAVALRY CAPTAIN A surprise, a piquant little surprise —
(*silence*)
FAIRY KING Maxim's it is, then!
ALL Maxim's!
(*They march off, umbrellas unfurled and singing*)
Vindobona on the Danube so blue,
My heart never can weary of you.
Howe'er far from the Prater we roam
We feel your charms, calling us home.
Filled with laughter, rejoicing and song,
O Vienna, to you we belong.
You're the jewel in Austria's crown,
Shining afar, queen of all towns.

Miss Mizzi's taking Jean
For a night out on the town.
She's no back number yet,
She'll take what she can get
With all those naughty ladies
Who whoop it up at Brady's.
Just see her let off steam
When she gets to Maxim's.

Let's open up another flask, hollodero.
It doesn't have to be the last, hollodero.
And when the wine in that's all gone, hollodero,

We'll go and get another one, we'll get another one.

Gong. The scene changes to Maxim's, with a bar and alcoves for the customers; at the back is a cabaret stage with a broad apron. They close their umbrellas and sit down at the tables; everyone is in very high spirits.

MC (*coming out from behind the curtain*) Ladies and gentlemen! What a charming audience. Such delightful ladies — and even more delightful gentlemen.
MATILDA (*gives a wolf whistle — general laughter*)
MC I'd like to give you a very warm welcome in the name of all of us here at Maxim's. Wasn't it the divine Shakespeare who said "All the world's a stage"? Here at Maxim's we take that as our motto, ladies and gentlemen. A world of enchantment on our stage for you. And now, for our next number will you take a trip with me down memory lane! (*exit*)

Fanfare — applause. The curtain rises to show Schönbrunn palace; to the strains of the "Hoch- und Deutschmeister March" a platoon of girls marches onto the stage, down into the audience, and back up on stage again. They are dressed in frilly underwear, boots, and old-fashioned helmets; their "captain" is carrying a sword, the others rifles; the "captain" directs the chorus girls in a shrill soprano with commands such as "Right face! Left face! Attention! Take aim! Fire! About face! Forward bend! Fall in! Present arms!" She walks up and down, inspecting her troops — frenzied applause from the audience; then she marches them off again, the girls singing, "We are the royal and imperial regiment Hoch- und Deutschmeister number four — mind the door," to the tune of the "Hoch- und Deutschmeister March." Curtain. The audience goes berserk. The orchestra plays the "Radetzky March."

FAIRY KING (*to the* CAVALRY CAPTAIN) What is all this nonsense sir? We humans are related to animals, no shadow of doubt about it.
CAVALRY CAPTAIN That's a matter of opinion.

FAIRY KING You still believe in Adam and Eve, then?
CAVALRY CAPTAIN Who knows?
THE AMERICAN (*to Mathilda*) You little wildcat, you!
FAIRY KING Wildcat! Or a leopard, even.
MATHILDA Cheers, Fairy King.
FAIRY KING The Captain's a mythical beast, there's something of a kangaroo about you and our American friend here's a miniature pinscher.
THE AMERICAN (*doesn't laugh at all*)Very amusing, very witty, I'm sure.
FAIRY KING And me? What am I?
MATHILDA A stag! With horns! Cheers, old stag!
(*roars of laughter; the internal telephone on the table rings — silence*)
FAIRY KING (*answers*) Yes? Whao's that? — What? — Honey? I don't know any Honey. — Oh, I see! Yes, certainly, that's me. Uncle speaking. — You want me to —? — You saucy little miss! — Where? At the bar? In the green dress? — What!? Still a virgin? And you ask your uncle to believe that? I'll have to come and check. (*makes a kissing noise at the receiver, puts it down, and empties a glass of the champagne the American ordered*)
MATHILDA Don't drink so much, Leopold.
FAIRY KING Go jump in a lake. (*stands up*) Alcohol's the only pleasure we oldies have left. Where's the bar?
MATHILDA What bar?
FAIRY KING Where's the bar, for Christ's sake!?
CAVALRY CAPTAIN I'll show you.
FAIRY KING I can find it myself. I don't need a chaperon. OK then, come on, show me the way. (*The Captain takes him to the bar, where two girls are waiting for him; the one in the green dress puts her arm round him straight away; the Captain stays at the bar too.*)
THE AMERICAN (*to Mathilda*) Who is that man, anyway?
MATHILDA A fairy king.
THE AMERICAN Oh!
MATHILDA Yes. You don't meet many men like him nowadays. Modest and decent, one of the old school. They're a dying breed.

THE AMERICAN More's the pity.
MATHILDA Today, unfortunately, he's rather sozzled —
THE AMERICAN There you go again. The way you put it! So charming! Over there in America everything's quite brutal.
(*pause*)
MATHILDA What do you weigh?
THE AMERICAN Two hundred and eighteen pounds.
MATHILDA My God!
THE AMERICAN May I be frank with you?
MATHILDA Be my guest.
THE AMERICAN I'm a complicated character.
MATHILDA How do you mean?
THE AMERICAN I've gone all dead inside, in here. I can only do it with prostitutes now — it comes from all the disappointments I've had.
MATHILDA Incredible. Such a sensitive soul in such a powerful body —
THE AMERICAN I was born under Saturn.
MATHILDA Oh, those planets! We're stuck with them and we can't do anything about it.
(*gong*)

MC (*comes out in front of the curtain*) Ladies and gentlemen! Now we present another magnificent number! The tableaux you are about to see have all been designed by leading artists — yes, artists! But you don't want to hear any more from me, you can judge for yourselves when you see our sensational, highly artistic, live-nude sculpture gallery! First tableau: Danube water-nymphs! Music, maestro, please!
(*The band strikes up the waltz "The Blue Danube" as the auditorium lights are dimmed. The curtains part to reveal three girls, naked from the waist up, with their legs in mermaid's tails. One is holding a lyre and the three are picturesquely posed in front of a black curtain with green lighting;. From the bar the voice of the Fairy King can be heard saying, "Naked as nature intended! That's what I like to see!" The curtains close to vigorous applause. Gong.*)

MC (*coming out in front of the curtain again*) Second tableau: our Zeppelin!
(*cheers*)
MC Music, maestro, please!
(*The band plays the march, "Fridericus Rex" and the curtains open to reveal three naked girls on the stage, one holding a propeller, the second a globe and the third a model Zeppelin. The audience goes wild, stands up and sings the first verse of "Deutschland über alles" before sitting down again. Gong.*)
MC (*coming out in front of the curtain again*) And now, ladies and gentlemen, our third tableau: The Pursuit of Fortune!
(*deathly silence*)
MC Maestro —
(*Now the band plays Schumann's "Reverie" and the curtains part for the third time to reveal a group of naked girls trampling over each other as they run after a golden ball on which Fortune is standing on one leg. Fortune is naked, too, and is called Marianne.*
MATHILDA Marianne! Jesus and Mary! Marianne!
MARIANNE (*starts, wobbles, can't keep her balance and has to get down off the golden ball; she stands staring at the audience, dazzled by the spotlights*)
THE AMERICAN What's all this about?
MATHILDA (*getting worked up*) Marianne! Marianne! Marianne!
THE AMERICAN (*angry*) Stop shouting. Have you gone crazy?!
MATHILDA Marianne!
THE AMERICAN Shut up! I'll give you Marianne! (*punches her in the chest*)
MATHILDA (*screams*)
The audience gets agitated, cries of "Lights, lights!")
MC (*dashes onto the stage*) Curtains! What's going on? Lights! Curtains! Lights!
(*As the curtains close, Marianne is still staring fixedly at the audience; the other girls have run off in confusion. Now the lights go up in the audience and there is a deathly hush for a moment again. Everyone is staring at Mathilda who is lying face down on the table, sobbing and crying in drunken hysteria.*

Tales from the Vienna Woods 107

FAIRY KING (*standing at the bar, pressing his hand to his heart*)
MATHILDA (*whimpering*) Marianne — Marianne — dear little Marianne — oh, oh, oh — I've known her since she was five years old.
MC Who's that she's going on about?
THE AMERICAN No idea.
MC Hysterical?
THE AMERICAN Epileptic!
A VOICE (*still in easy-going Viennese tones*) Throw the drunken bitch out.
MATHILDA I'm not drunk. No, I'm not, no, no, no. (*jumps up and tries to run out, but stumbles over her own feet and falls down, knocking the table over in the process. She is bruised and bleeding*) No, no, It's more than flesh and blood can stand. I'm not made of stone, I can't take any more, I can't take any more. (*dashes out, screaming*)
ALL (*apart from the Fairy King, watch her leave with baffled looks on their faces. Silence, then the gong*)
MC (*jumping up onto a chair*) Ladies and gentlemen! Ladies and gentlemen! That was the end of the official program. And now the unofficial part is about to commence — in the bar! (*dance music comes from the bar*) I'd just like to thank you all for being such a delightful audience. I hope you enjoy the rest of the evening. Good night, ladies and gentlemen.
(*The room gradually empties.*)
FAIRY KING Captain —
CAVALRY CAPTAIN Yes?
FAIRY KING So that's why you wanted us to come here instead of the Moulin Bleu, that was your "piquant little surprise." I had a sort of premonition at the time — a funny feeling there was something horrible in store for me —
CAVALRY CAPTAIN Yes, I did know Marianne was appearing here, I've been here quite often in fact, the last time was only yesterday. I think this has been going on far too long, you've hardened your heart —
FAIRY KING You've no right to meddle in other people's family affairs, you — soldier you!

CAVALRY CAPTAIN I feel it's my duty as a human being —
FAIRY KING (*interrupting*) What's that when it's at home?
CAVALRY CAPTAIN You can't be a real human being with real human feelings!
FAIRY KING Oh yes, very nice, very nice! And what am I supposed to be if I'm not a human being? A beast? You'd like that, wouldn't you? But I'm not a beast and I don't have a daughter!
CAVALRY CAPTAIN In that case I can see no point in staying here any longer. (*gives a stiff bow and leaves*)
FAIRY KING Well I can see a point! Hey, Mr. America, the world might blow up tomorrow, but do I care! I feel like writing picture postcards so people'll go green with envy when I tell them how much I'm enjoying myself.
THE AMERICAN Picture postcards! What a great idea! Brilliant! Postcards, postcards! (*buys a whole pile from a girl, sits down at one of the tables at the back and starts to write. He and the Fairy King are alone in the room; dance music can be heard from the bar.*)
MARIANNE (*comes in slowly in a bathrobe and stands in front of the Fairy King*)
FAIRY KING (*stares at her, looks her up and down — and turns his back on her.*
Silence)
MARIANNE Why didn't you read my letters? I wrote you three letters, but you didn't even open them, you had the mailman send them back.
(*silence*)
I wrote to tell you he'd left me —
FAIRY KING (*slowly turns round to face her and gives her a spiteful look*) I know. (*turns his back to her again*)
silence.
MARIANNE You know I have a child —?
FAIRY KING Of course.
(*silence*)
MARIANNE Things are pretty hard for the two of us, the boy and me —

Tales from the Vienna Woods 109

FAIRY KING You get what you deserve if you don't listen to people. That's enough now. (*stands up but has to sit down again*)
MARIANNE You're drunk, Papa —
FAIRY KING You just watch your mouth! Once and for all, I'm not your Papa! And watch your mouth, otherwise — (*makes a gesture of boxing her ears*) You should think of your poor dear mother. The dead can hear everything!
MARIANNE If Mommy were still alive —
FAIRY KING You leave your Mommy out of this, if you please! If she'd see you, standing there on the stage without a stitch on — for all and sundry to see! Have you no sense of shame? Disgusting!
MARIANNE I can't afford to feel ashamed.
(*silence; the music in the bar has also stopped*)
MARIANNE I earn two schillings a day here. It's not much, for the boy and me, but what else is there I can do? You refused to let me learn anything, not even my eurythmics. You brought me up to be a housewife, that's all —
FAIRY KING So it's all my fault then, is it? Wretched girl!
MARIANNE Papa, listen —
FAIRY KING (*interrupts her*) I'm no one's Papa!
MARIANNE (*strikes the table with her fist*) Stop it! You are my Papa, who else? And just listen for a moment. If this goes on for much longer — I can't earn any money, and I can't go on the streets — I just can't, I've tried, but I can't, I can only give myself to a man I really love, and as a woman with no qualifications I've nothing else to offer — there'll be nothing for it but the train.
FAIRY KING The train? What do you mean, the train?
MARIANNE The train. You travel on it. I'll throw myself under the train.
FAIRY KING You'll —? You'd do that to me as well, would you? (*suddenly starts to cry*) Oh you lousy bitch! Here I am, in the twilight of my years, and what do I get from you? One disgrace after another! Whatever have I done to deserve it!
MARIANNE (*sharply*) You just think of yourself all the time!
FAIRY KING (*stops crying and stares at her; loses his temper*) Go and throw yourself under a train, then! Go on, do it, together with

your little bastard! — Oh, I feel sick, sick, if only I could spew it all up! (*bends down over the table*)
MARIANNE (*looks at him; dance music comes from the bar again; she suddenly turns to leave*)
THE AMERICAN (*bars her way; he has finished writing his postcards*) Aha, our prima ballerina! (*looks at her with a smile*) Say — you wouldn't happen to have any stamps on you?
MARIANNE No.
THE AMERICAN (*speaking slowly*) You see I need ten twenty-groschen stamps and I'm willing to pay fifty schillings for them. (*pause*)
THE AMERICAN Sixty.
(*pause*)
THE AMERICAN (*taking out his wallet*) There's the Austrian schillings and there's the dollars —
MARIANNE Show me.
THE AMERICAN (*hands her his wallet. Pause.*)
MARIANNE Sixty?
THE AMERICAN Sixty-five.
MARIANNE That's a lot of money.
THE AMERICAN It's got to be earned.
(*Silence; the dance music has finished.*)
MARIANNE No thanks. (*hands him back his wallet*)
THE AMERICAN What do you mean?
MARIANNE I can't. You've got me wrong —
THE AMERICAN (*suddenly grabs her by the wrist and bellows*) Stop! That's my money you're stealing! Stop thief, whore! Open your hand, open it!
MARIANNE Ow!
THE AMERICAN There! A hundred schillings! Did you think I wouldn't notice, you stupid tart? (*slaps her*) Police! Police!
ALL (*appear in the doorway*)
FAIRY KING What's up, for Christ's sake?
THE AMERICAN That whore there's robbed me. A hundred schillings she stole! A hundred schillings! Police!
FAIRY KING But that's impossible — Marianne!

MARIANNE (*tearing herself free from the American*) Stop hitting me! I want you to stop hitting me!
FAIRY KING (*his hand over his heart*) One more thing! (*collapses*)
MC Water! Water! (*fusses round the Fairy King*)
(*silence*)
THE AMERICAN What's wrong? Doesn't he feel well?
MC No. That's a stroke!
MARIANNE (*cries out*) Papa! Papa!

End of Scene Five

SCENE SIX

Back in the quiet street in the Eighth District once more. It's Sunday and the stores are closed. Two "For rent" notices are stuck on the empty shop-window of the doll hospital. There is a wheelchair by the door.
Mathilda, with a posy of lilies of the valley, and the Cavalry Captain happen to meet outside the doll hospital, of all places.

CAVALRY CAPTAIN It's Sunday, Mathilda. And tomorrow's Monday again.
MATHILDA That's life, Captain.
CAVALRY CAPTAIN My conscience is clear, and yet — When there was all that fuss at Maxim's my motives were completely altruistic. I wanted to bring about a reconciliation, a reconciliation, and all we have is one tragedy after another. Poor Marianne's been locked up and the Fairy King's had a stroke. At least he's still alive.
MATHILDA (*pointing at the wheelchair*) Do you call that living?
CAVALRY CAPTAIN Death would be kinder.
(*silence*)
MATHILDA The first three days after he had his stroke, the specialist said it would take a miracle — Leopold could already hear the music of the spheres —
CAVALRY CAPTAIN Who's Leopold?
MATHILDA The Fairy King, of course.
CAVALRY CAPTAIN He's called Leopold too? My name's Leopold, you know —
MATHILDA Isn't that funny.
CAVALRY CAPTAIN What did you mean when you said he could hear the music of the spheres?
MATHILDA When a person's at death's door, his poor soul starts to leave his body — but only half his soul, and it flies up and up, higher and higher, to where there's this strange melody, that's the music of the spheres.
(*pause*)
CAVALRY CAPTAIN It's possible. As an idea — Where did you get those lovely lilies of the valley?

MATHILDA I'm afraid I just kind of took them, from Count Erdödy's park. I'm going to give them to poor Leopold, he likes flowers so much.
CAVALRY CAPTAIN Is he still angry with me?
MATHILDA Whatever for?
CAVALRY CAPTAIN Well, you know, because of the embarrassing situation I got him into at Maxim's.
MATHILDA Don't you worry your head about that, Captain. After all the poor man's been through, the last thing he wants to do is to get angry with you. Anyway, he's much more easygoing now. He's a broken man, that's what it is. When you can hardly walk or speak —
CAVALRY CAPTAIN Have you heard from Marianne?
(*silence*)
MATHILDA You can keep a secret, Captain?
CAVALRY CAPTAIN Of course.
MATHILDA Word of honor?
CAVALRY CAPTAIN If an old CAVALRY CAPTAIN can't keep his mouth closed — Just think of all the military secrets I know!
(*silence*)
MATHILDA She was here, Captain. Marianne came to see me. She spent three months in prison, including the time she was awaiting trial, and when she came out she'd nothing to eat — apart from her pride, that is, she still had that. But I soon knocked it out of her, and a thorough job I made of it, I can tell you. Just leave it to me, Captain, I'll get them to make it up, we women understand these things better than you men. You think you just have to wave your magic wand. You were much too direct at Maxim's — my God, didn't it give me a shock!
CAVALRY CAPTAIN All's well that ends well then. I'm off to the café now. I wish you good day. (*exit*)
ERIC (*appears on the Fairy King's balcony and waters the flowers*)
MATHILDA (*sees him*)
ERIC (*catches sight of Mathilda*) Good morning, madam.
MATHILDA If I'd known you were up there I'd have come later.
ERIC As soon as you come, I'll go — word of honor!

MATHILDA Off you go then. Go!

ERIC One moment please. (*takes a long time carefully watering a dead stalk, grinning spitefully as he does so, then he leaves the balcony*)

MATHILDA (*alone*) Lousy swine. Bastard. Pimp. Mangy cur —

ERIC (*comes out of doll hospital and gives her an exaggeratedly polite greeting*) Do excuse me, but I just wanted to let you know that this is probably the last time we'll see each other —

MATHILDA I should hope so!

ERIC You see, I'm leaving tomorrow — for good.

MATHILDA Bon voyage.

ERIC Thank you. (*doffs his hat politely and turns to go*)

MATHILDA (*suddenly*) Stop!

ERIC Madam?

(*silence*)

MATHILDA We can't say goodbye like this. Let's shake hands and part good friends.

ERIC Very well. (*shakes her hand then takes out a notebook and leafs through it*) I've got it all down here, the final balance, the whole sum, every single cigarette —

MATHILDA (*in a friendly voice*) I don't want your cigarettes —

ERIC A matter of honor!

MATHILDA (*takes the hand in which he is holding the notebook and caresses it*) Your trouble is you know nothing about psychology, Eric — (*gives him a friendly nod and goes off slowly into the doll hospital*)

ERIC (*watches her leave; alone*) Fifty-year-old piece of shit! (*exit*)

(*The schoolgirl on the second floor starts to play again, "Tales from the Vienna Woods" by Johann Strauss.*)

OSCAR (*enters with Alfred, pointing to the wheelchair*) His new limousine —

ALFRED A stroke like that's no joke. What's this? "For rent?"

OSCAR (*with a smile*) That too. Run out of magic. Unless, that is, he makes it up with Marianne.

ALFRED Isn't it sad. This whole tragic affair's no fault of mine, you know. Looking back, I just can't understand what I thought I was doing. Everything used to be fine, I had no worries, not a care in the world — and then you let yourself get involved in some affair — Serves me right, I suppose, devil only knows what got into me.

OSCAR True love, the real thing —

ALFRED No, no! That's not me at all! I was too soft, that's what it was. I just can't say no, and a relationship like that automatically goes from bad to worse. I didn't want to break up your engagement, but our dear Marianne had this all-or-nothing attitude. You know what I mean?

OSCAR I certainly do. Men only appear to be the active partners, women the passive ones. When you take a closer look —

ALFRED — you find yourself staring into unfathomable depths.

OSCAR You see?! That's why I never held it against you personally. I never wished you any harm.

ALFRED But Marianne?

OSCAR (*smiles*) Yes, she's paid for it dearly, the poor thing. For her great passion —

ALFRED But to bring tragedy to so many people. — We men really ought to stick together more.

OSCAR We're just too naive.

ALFRED Too true.

(*pause*)

ALFRED Oscar, I don't know how to thank you for offering to patch things up between Mathilda and me —

OSCAR (*interrupts*) Shh!

MATHILDA (*comes out of the doll hospital with the Fairy King; he is using two sticks and seems to be almost completely paralyzed, he can only use his arms; she gets him settled in his wheelchair, tucks in a blanket round his legs and places the lilies of the valley in his lap — the waltz breaks off in the middle of a bar*) There we are, now we're all ready for a walk. But don't stay out too long, and take care, d'you hear? I'll be back in half an hour. It's probably best if you just go as far as the playground and then come back — (*sees Oscar — Alfred hid in the doorway of the butcher's while she was occupied with the Fairy king*) Ah, Oscar. Good morning, Oscar.

OSCAR Good morning.

MATHILDA Did you hear that, Leopold? Your friend Oscar's here. Oscar.

FAIRY KING (*nods*)

MATHILDA (*to Oscar*) We feel a lot better today, things are looking up. We just have to avoid any excitement, the least excitement could mean another stroke and then — (*to the Fairy King*) D'you hear that? No getting excited, right? Shh now, not a word. It just tires you out. Off you go, I'll see you in half an hour. And don't lose my lilies of the valley.

FAIRY KING (*goes off in his wheelchair*)

OSCAR Very touching, the way you look after our invalid.

MATHILDA I'm the only one there is to look after him. It's part of a woman's nature, a kind of motherly instinct (*takes out a pocket mirror and repairs her make-up*) Oscar, I'm gradually getting him under my thumb, because he's come to depend on me — and I'll get him to make it up with Marianne. And he will make it up, even if only for fear of a second stroke. That's what I'm basing my plan on, his fear of another stroke. You'll see, I'll have this little despot eating out of my hand yet.

OSCAR Mathilda, there's someone who wants to make it up with you.

MATHILDA Who? Eric?

OSCAR No.

MATHILDA Who then?

OSCAR Over there —

MATHILDA (*goes over to the butcher's and sees Alfred*)

ALFRED (*raises his hat*)

(*silence*)

MATHILDA Oh.

ALFRED I beg you to forgive me.

(*silence*)

You can't imagine what it cost me to say how sorry I am, to eat humble pie like this. But I know I've wronged you, and that's stronger than my sense of shame —

MATHILDA Wronged me?

ALFRED Yes.

MATHILDA When?

ALFRED (*baffled*)
MATHILDA You haven't behaved badly toward me.
ALFRED (*even more baffled; with an embarrassed smile*) But I left you —
MATHILDA You left me? I left you! And anyway, that wasn't bad, that was good, very good, I'll have you know, you conceited clown.
ALFRED We parted good friends. remember!
MATHILDA It's all over between us, understand? In future I don't want to have anything to do with an absolute swine.
(*silence*)
ALFRED What do you mean, an absolute swine? You've just said yourself I didn't behave badly toward you?
MATHILDA Not toward me. But toward Marianne! And your child!
(*silence*)
ALFRED Marianne always said I could hypnotize people. (*shouts at her*) How can I help it if I have this effect on women?!
MATHILDA Don't shout at me.
OSCAR In my opinion Alfred behaved quite well toward Marianne —

MATHILDA Men! There you go, sticking up for each other again! Well I've got my own feminine solidarity. (*to Alfred*) I'll cut you down to size till you feel so small.
(*silence*)
ALFRED I lay down my arms. You don't have to tell me I'm no good, I well aware of it myself. It's because I'm weak. I need to have someone I can look after, someone I have to look after, otherwise it's downhill all the way with me. But I couldn't look after Marianne, that's what was wrong. — If I'd had some capital I could have gone back to the horses, even though she wouldn't let me —
MATHILDA She wouldn't let you?
ALFRED For reasons of morality.
MATHILDA That was stupid. That's the one thing you can do!
ALFRED You see! That was the attitude that ruined our relationship! That and that alone!
MATHILDA Don't lie.

(*silence*)
ALFRED Mathilda! I tried selling skin cream, fountain pens, Persian carpets — and I made a mess of it and now I'm in a real spot. You used to be so understanding —
MATHILDA (*interrupts him*) What would you do if I were to lend you fifty schillings?
(*silence*)
ALFRED Fifty?
MATHILDA Fifty.
ALFRED I'd wire Maisons-Lafitte right away, an each-way bet —
MATHILDA (*interrupting him*) And? And?
ALFRED What do you mean?
MATHILDA And your winnings?
(*silence*)
ALFRED (*with a sly grin*) Any winnings I would hand over personally to my son tomorrow.
MATHILDA We'll see, we'll see.
MARIANNE (*comes on quickly then pulls up with a start when she sees the others*)
OSCAR Marianne!
MATHILDA There you are!
MARIANNE (*stares at them one after the other, then quickly turns to leave*)
MATHILDA Hold it! Stay right there! We're going to clean up all the dirt here — we're going to have a good clear out — we're all going to make up and be friends, whether you like it or not!
(*silence*)
OSCAR Marianne, I'm happy to forgive you everything you've done to me — loving brings greater happiness than being loved. — If you have one spark of real feeling left in you, then you must be aware that I'd marry you today, in spite of everything, if you were still free — — I'm talking about the child —
(*silence*)
MARIANNE What are you saying about it?
OSCAR (*with a smile*) I'm sorry.
MARIANNE What?
OSCAR About the child —

(*silence*)
MARIANNE Leave the child in peace. What's the child ever done to you? And don't keep looking at me like that.
MATHILDA Marianne, this is supposed to be a reconciliation.
MARIANNE (*pointing at Alfred*) But not with him.
MATHILDA With him too. It's all or nothing. Even that thing (*also pointing at Alfred*) is only human.
ALFRED Well thank you very much.
MARIANNE Only yesterday you were saying he was a filthy beast.
MATHILDA Yesterday was yesterday and today's today — and anyway, you stick to your own affairs.
ALFRED As Nietzsche says, "Only a changed man can be the same to me."
OSCAR (*to Marianne*) Or as Goethe put it, "Die and be transformed."
MARIANNE (*grinning*) God, aren't we cultured!
OSCAR They're just mottoes we got from the calendar.
MATHILDA Mottoes or not, he's just a human being with all his inborn faults and vices — You can't have given him enough moral support, that's the problem.
MARIANNE I did what I could.
MATHILDA You're just too young, that's what it is.
(*silence*)
ALFRED When all's said and done, I was no angel.
MATHILDA When all's said and done, no one's ever to blame in that kind of relationship — when all's said and done, it's a question of your planets, the way your influences influence each other, that kind of thing —
MARIANNE But they locked me up.
(*silence*)
It was very humiliating.
OSCAR The police can't treat everyone with kid gloves.
MATHILDA I hope they were female officers at least?
MARIANNE Some of them.
FAIRY KING (*comes on in his wheelchair, his jaw drops and he brakes sharply*)

MATHILDA (*runs to him, bends over him, caresses him, and talks to him as if he were a little child*) Now then, now then, now then — don't get worked up, don't get worked up — and who's this then, who's this? — it's our little Marianne, little Marianne, yes, little Marianne — Leopold, it's a sign from God, the fact that you're still with us — Shhh! Don't get worked up, don't get worked up — otherwise there'll be another stroke, another stroke, and what then? Shh! Come on now, make it up, make it up — then you can keep running the store, and everything will be all right, all right, all right —
FAIRY KING (*pushes Mathilda aside and stares at Marianne and Alfred*)
(*silence*)
ALFRED (*raises his hat*)
MARIANNE Hello —
(*silence*)
FAIRY KING (*the left side of his face is paralyzed, giving him a speech impediment*) Hello.
MARIANNE (*starts and stares at him in horror*)
FAIRY KING (*to Mathilda*) What's the matter with her?
(*silence*)
FAIRY KING Oh, I see — my modern enunciation — that's what happens — the good Lord in his wisdom —
(*silence*)
FAIRY KING What's she staring at me like that for? Stop making me get worked up, you stupid bitch.
MARIANNE Poor Papa! My poor Papa! (*rushes over to him, falls to her knees and buries her head in his lap, sobbing softly*)
FAIRY KING (*deeply moved; slowly runs his fingers through her hair*) Marianne! My Marianne! You silly girl! Silly girl! (*suddenly stops and pushes Marianne aside*) What's this? What's this? (*gets jerkily to his feet*) I think I can walk again. (*tries to, leaning on his stick, and manages*)
MATHILDA A miracle! A miracle —
FAIRY KING (*walking up and down*) I can walk again! I can walk again!
MATHILDA There you are, see what a good deed you've done.

FAIRY KING It's all in the nerves really, these strokes —
OSCAR And the shock of this joyful —
FAIRY KING (*interrupts him*) Yes, yes! A new man! A phoenix! (*tears down the "For rent" sign with his stick*) Well done, Marianne, well done! You were indirectly responsible. (*pinches her cheek*) And tomorrow — (*very slowly*) and tomorrow, tomorrow Grandpapa will go and see his darling boy — (*sings*) His darling boy, his darling boy. (*grins and gives Marianne a thwack on the behind with his stick*)
MARIANNE Ouch! (*laughs joyfully*)

End of Scene Six

SCENE SEVEN

Out in the Wachau, where green the wine grows.
A cottage below a ruined castle.
The Daughter is hanging up the washing, the Mother is peeling potatoes, and the Grandmother is sitting in the sun at a little table tuning her zither. Somewhere nearby the Blue Danube is flowing past.

ALFRED (*enters; looks round as if he is looking for something, tips his hat to the Daughter*)
THE DAUGHTER (*acknowledges his greeting, leaves the washing and goes up to him*) Have you come to go up the tower, sir?
ALFRED What tower?
THE DAUGHTER (*points*) Our tower. — The climb is well worth the effort, which is rewarded with magnificent views and an instructive panorama. If you want I'll guide you, sir.
ALFRED (*with a blasé smile*) And how much does it cost?
THE DAUGHTER Twenty groschen.
(*pause*)
ALFRED Who does the ruin belong to?
THE DAUGHTER The state. We're just the wardens. But at night I wouldn't go up there for all the money in the world. The ghosts come to frighten people.
ALFRED What ghosts?
THE DAUGHTER Well, a kind of Bluebeard who murdered his wives in their beds with a shovel.
ALFRED (*with another blasé smile*) Not all of us poor men do that to their wives in bed, you know —
THE DAUGHTER Ooh, you are —
THE MOTHER (*calls to her*) Julie! What does the gentleman want?
THE DAUGHTER He wants to go up our tower.
THE MOTHER Oh, that's different.
ALFRED That wasn't what I came for, but with such a charming guide — (*follows the Daughter into the ruin*)
THE GRANDMOTHER Frieda!
THE MOTHER Yes mama?

Tales from the Vienna Woods 123

THE GRANDMOTHER I'm not happy with Julie.
THE MOTHER For goodness sake, mama, neither am I —
THE GRANDMOTHER A fine daughter you've got there — saucy and lazy. Just like her father.
THE MOTHER Can't you leave the man in peace! He's been six feet under for ten years now and you still can't leave him in peace.
THE GRANDMOTHER And what was it put him there in the first place? Was it me? Or was it the drink? The whole of your dowry went down his throat.
THE MOTHER I don't want to hear any more of that, I've had enough.
THE GRANDMOTHER Shut your face. (*plays "Under the Double Eagle" on her zither*)
THE DAUGHTER (*appears at the top of the tower with Alfred*)
ALFRED (*listens*) That's nice. Who's that playing?
THE DAUGHTER That's my grandmother.
ALFRED Your grandmother? Must be some lady!
THE DAUGHTER Well she plays a different tune with me, I can tell you. I won't stand for any of her nonsense. And keep your hands to yourself, if you please.
(*pause*)
ALFRED She plays with plenty of feeling.
THE DAUGHTER She only plays when she's in a bad mood.
ALFRED What's got into her, then?
THE DAUGHTER A tragic accident. Yesterday.
ALFRED (*with a smile*) Very tragic?
THE DAUGHTER Let's talk of something else, shall we. — Don't do that —
THE GRANDMOTHER (*the march is finished*)Frieda! Have you written that letter?
THE MOTHER No.
THE GRANDMOTHER D'you want me to write it then?
THE MOTHER No, I'll do it, when I get round to it. Oh, isn't it just awful! And she'll blame us for not taking proper care.
THE GRANDMOTHER Us? You, you mean. You.
THE MOTHER Why me?

THE GRANDMOTHER Was it my idea to take in a child? No, it was your idea. You kept saying you liked the idea of having a little darling to care for. That's what you said! I was against it, right from the start. All you get is trouble. For a lousy fifteen schillings a month.

THE MOTHER Okay, okay. It's all my fault as usual. Fine. And it's my fault the kid fell into the Danube yesterday? — It's my fault he drowned, is it?

THE GRANDMOTHER (*says nothing but gives her a spiteful look and starts to play the "Danube Waves" waltz*)

THE MOTHER (*watches her, full of hatred*) Old cow! (*makes a furious exit, taking the potatoes into the cottage*)

ALFRED It's beautiful, isn't it, our dear old Danube. Just look at the way it flows — beautiful, beautiful.

THE DAUGHTER I wish I were in Vienna.

ALFRED And I wish I could stay out here for ever — a quiet life, in a quiet little cottage like this, no noise —

THE DAUGHTER What can you make of your life out here?

ALFRED What have I made of my life in Vienna?

THE DAUGHTER I'd know what to do if I were in Vienna. I'd manage.

ALFRED There'd be no escape, even for you.

THE DAUGHTER Escape from what?

ALFRED Men.

THE DAUGHTER Huh, they'd better watch out for me!

ALFRED Some woman, eh? Just like your dear old granny. (*pause*)

THE DAUGHTER What are you doing out here anyway, a handsome city slicker like you?

ALFRED I was looking for a house. Number seventeen.

THE DAUGHTER Number seventeen?

THE GRANDMOTHER (*stops playing the zither and starts to knit*)

ALFRED Yes. They're looking after a kid, a little boy. And I'm the proud father. — What are you looking at me like that for?

THE DAUGHTER (*slowly*) You're the father?

ALFRED (*with a smile*) The very same.

THE DAUGHTER The kid's father?

Tales from the Vienna Woods 125

ALFRED You don't think I look like a father? Or have you heard things about me already? Is that why you're giving me that funny look? Has the kid's mama been saying things about me? We've separated, you see —
THE DAUGHTER It's awful, really awful —
ALFRED What's wrong?
(*silence*)
THE DAUGHTER No, I can't bring myself to say it, I can't —
ALFRED Look at me.
THE DAUGHTER (*looks at him*) I can't look you in the eyes and —
ALFRED But I can see myself in your eyes —
THE DAUGHTER That house down there, our house, that's number seventeen — and there was a terrible accident — yesterday —
ALFRED What?
THE DAUGHTER To the kid — to your kid — he was playing by the Danube — and he fell in —
ALFRED Dead?!
THE DAUGHTER Yes. Drowned.
(*silence*)
ALFRED In the Danube.
THE DAUGHTER And he was so sweet, our little boy — (*starts to cry*)
ALFRED (*puts his arms round her*) There, there, don't cry, don't cry —
THE DAUGHTER I don't know you — but you can't be all bad — it's you who's the father, I'm not even related, and yet you're comforting me —
(*silence*)
ALFRED How big was the kid?
THE DAUGHTER That big —
(*silence*)
ALFRED And his mother? Does she know yet?
THE DAUGHTER No, we can't bring ourselves to write to her — we all liked the little guy so much. Except grandmother. She had this feeling something would go wrong. She was against taking a child in, right from the start. Now she's crowing "I told you so," of course.

(*silence*)

ALFRED In the Danube. In our beautiful blue Danube —

THE DAUGHTER Look, there are the fishermen coming to search for the body.

FISHERMEN (*with long poles and grappling irons; they talk to the Mother, who has come out of the cottage again; the Grandmother listens*)

THE DAUGHTER Do you want to go back down?

ALFRED No. I'd like to be alone.

THE DAUGHTER Fate weaves our destiny and we can do nothing about it.

ALFRED I'm alone a lot.

THE DAUGHTER Me too.

THE FISHERMEN (*leave*)

THE MOTHER They've still not found anything.

THE GRANDMOTHER I'm not surprised.

THE MOTHER Nothing surprises you.

THE GRANDMOTHER Thank God.

(*silence*)

THE GRANDMOTHER Perhaps it's not such a terrible thing after all, perhaps it's all for the best — I mean for your young lady — I know that kind of young lady — perhaps she'll even be glad she's to be rid of it —

THE MOTHER Mama! Are you out of your mind?!

THE GRANDMOTHER You mind your tongue, bitch!

THE MOTHER No, you mind your tongue, monster! The girl's a mother, just like you.

THE GRANDMOTHER (*screeching*) Don't you go comparing her with me! My child was born on the right side of the blanket — or are you an illegitimate slut? Them that don't ask God's blessing can't expect any good to come of it. And why should they? Where would we be then, eh? (*plays her march, "Under the Double Eagle," again*)

THE MOTHER Don't start that again. Stop playing!

THE GRANDMOTHER Okay, then. But in that case that letter's going to get written. Now. And if you're too much of a coward, I'll dictate it to you. (*gets up*) Sit down. Here's pencil and paper. I've got it all worked out.

THE MOTHER Monster —

THE GRANDMOTHER Shut up, sit down, and write. You should be glad someone's doing the hard work for you.

THE MOTHER (*sits down*)

THE GRANDMOTHER (*walks up and down, her back bent, and dictates*) Dear Miss Whatever-she's-called — Yes, Miss! — Unfortunately we have some sad news for you. The Good Lord in His wisdom has taken your child from you. Yesterday the child was playing in the meadow by the Danube and fell in, full stop. You will find comfort in the thought that God loves innocent little children, full stop. No blame attaches to me or to my family — full stop. New paragraph. Together with my mother and my daughter, I offer you my most heartfelt condolences. End of letter. Yours sincerely etc, etc.

MARIANNE (*comes with the Fairy King, Mathilda, and Oscar; she has hurried on ahead of them*) Hello, Frau Kreutler. Good afternoon, grandmother. How are you today? I haven't been out here for such a long time. I'm just glad to see you all again. — This is my father.

FAIRY KING (*raises his hat*)

THE MOTHER (*gapes at him*)

MARIANNE (*suddenly senses something is wrong*) What's the matter with you?

THE GRANDMOTHER (*hands her the letter*)

MARIANNE (*takes it mechanically and looks around apprehensively*) Where's the kid? Where's the kid?

THE GRANDMOTHER Read the letter, please. Read it —

MARIANNE (*reads the letter*)

FAIRY KING Where is the little chap then? (*he has a toy in his hand with a bell attached; he jangles it*) Come on, my little cherub, Granpop's here. Granpop's here.

MARIANNE (*lets the letter fall*)

(*silence*)

FAIRY KING (*worried all of a sudden*) Marianne! Has something happened?

MATHILDA (*picks up the letter and reads it; screams*) Holy Mother of God! He's dead! He's gone! My little cherub! Dead!
FAIRY KING (*staggers, drops the toy and covers his face in his hands*)
(*silence*)
THE GRANDMOTHER (*picks up the toy and examines it with curiosity; jangles the bell*)
MARIANNE (*observes her; she suddenly gives a hoarse cry, falls on the Grandmother and tries to strike her down her with the zither.*
OSCAR (*grabs her by the throat and throttles her*)
MARIANNE (*makes gurgling noises and drops the zither*)
(*silence*)
THE GRANDMOTHER (*softly*) Slut. Animal. Jailbird. Try to kill me, would you? Me?
THE MOTHER (*suddenly screams at the Grandmother*) See that you get in the house! And be quick about it! Quick!
THE GRANDMOTHER (*goes up to the Mother slowly*) You've wanted me under the ground for ages — haven't you? But I'm not going just yet, not just yet — There! (*gives the Mother a slap across the face*) You'd all like to see me dead, would you? Well you can all rot in hell, the whole lot of you. (*goes into the cottage*)
(*silence*)
THE MOTHER (*sobbing*) You'll pay for that — (*follows the Grandmother*)
FAIRY KING (*slowly takes his hands away from his face*) Another stroke, another stroke — No, no, please God, don't take me. Please God. (*crosses himself*) Our father, who art in Heaven — the Lord is mighty and the Lord is just — you are just, aren't you Lord? Oh, don't take me, don't take me —— thou art just — thou art just —(*does up his tie and walks off slowly*)
MARIANNE I once asked God what His plans for me were, but He didn't tell me, otherwise I wouldn't still be here — He didn't tell me anything — He wanted to keep it as a surprise for me — the bastard!
OSCAR Marianne! Don't turn your face away from God.
MARIANNE The bastard! The bastard! (*spits*)

OSCAR Marianne, God knows what he's doing, you can believe me.
MARIANNE My kid! Where are you now, son?
OSCAR In paradise.
MARIANNE Stop tormenting me —
OSCAR I'm not a sadist! I'm just trying to comfort you. You still have your whole life in front of you. The Lord giveth and the Lord taketh away.
MARIANNE He's only taken away from me —
OSCAR God is love, Marianne, and God strikes those He loves.
MARIANNE He's thrashing me like a dog —
OSCAR That too. If it's necessary.
(*silence*)
OSCAR Marianne. I once told you I hoped you would never have to go through what you did to me — and in spite of that God has left you with people around you — people who love you in spite of everything — and now, now things have sorted themselves out — — I once told you you couldn't escape my love, Marianne —
MARIANNE I can't go on anymore — I just can't go on anymore —
OSCAR Come with me — (*supports her, kisses her on the mouth and goes off with her*)
ALFRED (*comes down from the tower with the Daughter*)
MATHILDA (*watches the Daughter go off*) Where have you been?
ALFRED Up the tower.
MATHILDA What kind of tower would that be?
ALFRED This isn't the time for stupid questions!
(*silence*)
MATHILDA I'm sorry. My condolences.
ALFRED Thanks.
(*silence*)
ALFRED (*taking money out of his pocket*) There. I wired my bet through yesterday and won at Maisons-Lafitte — eighty-four schillings — and I wanted to give it to my son —
MATHILDA We'll give him a lovely gravestone. A little kneeling angel, perhaps.
ALFRED I'm sad, very sad. I was just thinking — without children that's the end of you, you just die out. Pity.

It gets dark; a large string orchestra can be heard playing "Tales from the Vienna Woods." The scene changes for the final tableau, Oscar and Marianne's wedding celebrations in a kitschy baroque-style hall: formal entrance and solo dance by the bride and groom, then all join in the dancing; among the wedding guests are Mathilda, Alfred, Eric, the Cavalry Captain, both Aunts with all the relations, Havlichek in his Sunday best, the Father Confessor, the Grandmother, Mother and Daughter, the MC with the chorus girls and their boyfriends; they're all there, even the American, who presents a huge bouquet of white lilies to the bride; first and foremost, of course, the Fairy King. The curtain falls.

CAVALRY CAPTAIN (*appears in front of the curtain*) Ladies and gentlemen, I'm afraid there have been so many messages of congratulation that our happy couple, Oscar and Marianne, just have not time to get round to thanking everyone personally. The great honor, ladies and gentlemen, of thanking you all most heartily in the name of the newlyweds for your kind wishes of happiness has fallen to me. Thank you, ladies and gentlemen, thank you all.

End

Casimir and Caroline

Play

And love never ends
(1 Corinthians 13,8)

A score with the music for the songs in *Casimir and Caroline* is available from the holders of the performing rights, Thomas Sessler Verlag, Johannesgasse 12, A-1010 Vienna.

CHARACTERS

CASIMIR
CAROLINE
RAUCH
SPEER
BARKER
MIDGET
SCHÜRZINGER
FRANZ MERKL
MERKL'S GIRLFRIEND ERNA
ELLI
MARIA
MAN WITH THE HEAD OF A BULLDOG
JUANITA
FAT LADY
WAITRESS
FIRST-AID ATTENDANT
DOCTOR
FREAKS AND FAIRGROUND PEOPLE

The play takes place at the Oktoberfest, the Munich Beer Festival, during the Depression in the early thirties.

SCENE 1

As the lights go down in the auditorium the orchestra plays the Munich song "Solang der alte Peter."
The curtain rises.

SCENE 2

On the left is an ice-cream vendor selling Turkish delight and balloons, on the right a try-your-strength machine: if you ring the bell you get a medal, one for each time it rings.
It is already late in the afternoon and the Zeppelin is just flying low over the fairground — distant screams, a fanfare and a roll of drums.

SCENE 3

RAUCH Three cheers for the Zeppelin! Three cheers for Germany!
FAIRGROUND BARKER Heil!
SPEER Majestic! Hip, hip hooray!
(*silence*)
MIDGET When you think how far we humans have come already — (*waves his handkerchief*)
(*silence*)
CAROLINE It's going to disappear any moment now, the Zeppelin —
MIDGET On the horizon.
CAROLINE I can hardly see it anymore —
MIDGET I can still see it quite clearly.
CAROLINE Now it's gone. (*sees Casimir, smiles*) Hey, Casimir, soon we'll all be flying.
CASIMIR Well you can count me out. (*turns to the try-your-strength machine and hits the pin; a silent crowd is looking on with interest. He only rings the bell at the third attempt, then pays and gets his medal*)

CAROLINE Congratulations.
CASIMIR What for?
CAROLINE Your medal.
CASIMIR Oh. Thanks.
(*silence*)
CAROLINE The Zeppelin's flying as far as Oberammergau, but it's coming back and it's going to do a few loops above us.
CASIMIR So what? You've got twenty industrial fat cats flying round up there while a few million are starving down here. I don't give a shit for your Zeppelin! It's all a big con, I've worked it out ... the Zeppelin, don't you see, it's an airship, and when one of us sees this airship he feels as if he's flying in it — when all we have is down-at-heel shoes and nothing to get our teeth into but the table edge.
CAROLINE When you're sad it makes me sad too.
CASIMIR I'm not a sad person.
CAROLINE Oh yes you are. You're a pessimist.
CASIMIR Too true I am. Any intelligent person's a pessimist. (*turns away from her and goes back to the try-your-weight machine; this time he rings the bell three times, pays and gets three medals; then he goes over to Caroline again*) It's easy for you to laugh. I told you there was no way I was going to come to the Oktoberfest today. Redundant yesterday, dole tomorrow, but enjoy yourself today, even have a good laugh, maybe!
CAROLINE I wasn't laughing.
CASIMIR Of course you were laughing. It's OK for you to laugh, you're still earning, you live at home and your parents have their pensions. But my parents are dead and I'm alone in the world, completely alone.
(*silence*)
CAROLINE Perhaps we're wrong for each other, too heavy —
CASIMIR What do you mean by that?
CAROLINE Well, you're a pessimist and I have a melancholy streak too — — Just now, for example — when the Zeppelin was flying over —
CASIMIR Oh, you know what you can do with your Zeppelin!

CAROLINE Don't keep shouting at me like that, I've done nothing to deserve it.
CASIMIR Get stuffed. (*exit*)

SCENE 4

CAROLINE (*watches him go; then turns round slowly, goes to the ice-cream vendor, buys one and licks it thoughtfully*)
SCHÜRZINGER (*already licking his second ice*)
CAROLINE What are you looking at me like that for?
SCHÜRZINGER Pardon me, I was thinking of something quite different.
CAROLINE Exactly.
(*silence*)
SCHÜRZINGER I was just thinking about the Zeppelin.
(*silence*)
CAROLINE The Zeppelin's flying as far as Oberammergau.
SCHÜRZINGER Ever been to Oberammergau?
CAROLINE Three times.
SCHÜRZINGER Wow!
(*silence*)
CAROLINE But the people there aren't saints. People are bad everywhere.
SCHÜRZINGER You mustn't say that. People aren't good or bad. It's true, the current economic system forces them to be more selfish than they would be since they have to live from hand to mouth. D'you follow me?
CAROLINE No.
SCHÜRZINGER You will soon enough. Let's assume you're in love with a man and he loses his job. You'll start to fall out of love with him. It's automatic.
CAROLINE I can't believe that.
SCHÜRZINGER It's true!
CAROLINE Oh no it's not. If her man's in difficulties, any self-respecting woman will stick by him more than ever —— I would imagine.

SCHÜRZINGER I wouldn't.
(*silence*)
CAROLINE Can you read palms?
SCHÜRZINGER No.
CAROLINE What is it you do exactly?
SCHÜRZINGER Have a guess.
CAROLINE Precision engineer.
SCHÜRZINGER No. Tailor's cutter.
CAROLINE I'd never have thought that.
SCHÜRZINGER Why not?
CAROLINE Because I can't stand tailors. All tailors are big-headed.
(*silence*)
SCHÜRZINGER I'm an exception. I've thought a lot about destiny.
CAROLINE Do you like ice-cream?
SCHÜRZINGER My one passion?
CAROLINE Your only passion?
SCHÜRZINGER Yes.
CAROLINE Pity.
SCHÜRZINGER Why?
CAROLINE If that's the case you must have something missing.

SCENE 5

CASIMIR (*reappears and waves Caroline over*)
CAROLINE (*goes to him*)
CASIMIR Who's that you're talking to?
CAROLINE Someone I know.
CASIMIR Since when?
CAROLINE Oh, for ages. We just met by chance. — Don't you believe me?
CASIMIR Why shouldn't I believe you?
(*silence*)
CAROLINE What do you want?
(*silence*)
CASIMIR What did you mean just now when you said we were too heavy for each other?

CAROLINE (*a malevolent silence*)
CASIMIR Might that perhaps mean that we two might perhaps not be meant for each other?
CAROLINE Perhaps.
CASIMIR So that might perhaps mean that we should perhaps split up — and that you've been thinking about it?
CAROLINE Now's not the time to ask.
CASIMIR And why not, if I may ask?
CAROLINE Because I'm in a bad mood, and when I'm in that kind of mood I'm incapable of giving you a straight answer.
(*silence*)
CASIMIR You are, are you? Hmm. So that's the way it is, is it? They're all the same. No exceptions.
CAROLINE What on earth are you talking about?
CASIMIR That's the way it is.
CAROLINE (*staring at him*) What is?
(*silence*)
CASIMIR You don't think it's odd you suddenly realize we might perhaps not be suited to each other today of all days, the day I've been made redundant?
(*silence*)
CAROLINE I don't understand you, Casimir.
CASIMIR Just think. Just think about it, young lady.
(*silence*)
CAROLINE (*suddenly*) Oh you ungrateful wretch! Haven't I always stuck by you? Have you forgotten the problems I had with my parents because I didn't take one of those men with a good steady job with the state? Have you forgotten how I stuck by you and always took your side?
CASIMIR Don't get all worked up. Just think what you've done to me.
CAROLINE And what are you doing to me?
CASIMIR I'm acknowledging a fact, that's what I'm doing. And now I'm walking out on you — (*exit.*)

SCENE 6

CAROLINE (*watches him go, then turns back to Schürzinger; it is already starting to get dark*)
SCHÜRZINGER Who was that?
CAROLINE My fiancé.
SCHÜRZINGER You're engaged?
CAROLINE He's just been horrible to me. He lost his job yesterday and now he says I want to split up with him because he's lost his job.
SCHÜRZINGER The old, old story.
CAROLINE Let's talk about something else.
(*silence*)
SCHÜRZINGER He's standing over there watching us.
CAROLINE I'd like to have a go on the roller-coaster now.
SCHÜRZINGER It'll cost you.
CAROLINE But I've come to the fair and that's what I want to do. Come on, have a go with me.
SCHÜRZINGER Well, just this once.
CAROLINE That's up to you.
(*dark*)

SCENE 7

The orchestra plays the "Glowworm Idyll" from Paul Lincke's operetta Lysistrata.

SCENE 8

Beside the roller-coaster, at the end of the Oktoberfest field; a bit out of the way and not very well lit. It is already dark but in the distance everything is lit up.
Caroline and Schürzinger enter and listen to the roar of the roller-coaster and the rapturous shrieks of the people on it.

SCENE 9

CAROLINE Yes, that's the real genuine roller-coaster. There's another one but the ride's over in no time at all. That's where you get your tickets. Oops, something's come undone.
SCHÜRZINGER What?
CAROLINE I don't know yet. Turn round a moment, please.
(*silence*)
SCHÜRZINGER (*looking the other way*) Your fiancé's still following us. He's talking to someone, a man and a woman. They're not letting us out of their sight.
CAROLINE Where? —— That's Franz Merkl and his girl-friend Erna. Oh, I know him. He used to work with my Casimir but he's turned to crime. God knows how often he's been inside.
SCHÜRZINGER The small fry end up in jail and the big fish go free.
CAROLINE True enough, but Merkl beats Erna up, even though she never goes out of line. Hitting a weak woman, that's the absolute pits.
SCHÜRZINGER Definitely.
CAROLINE Casimir has a very violent temper too, but he's never touched me.
SCHÜRZINGER Let's hope he doesn't cause a fuss.
CAROLINE No, he never does that in public. He's got too much self-control. It's part of his job.
SCHÜRZINGER What is he then?
CAROLINE (*has finished adjusting whatever it was*) Driver. Chauffeur.
SCHÜRZINGER People with violent tempers are usually good-natured.
CAROLINE Are you afraid?
SCHÜRZINGER What makes you say that?
(*silence*)
CAROLINE Now I'm going on the roller-coaster. (*exit with Schürzinger, for a while there is no one to be seen on stage*)

SCENE 10

CASIMIR (*enters slowly with Franz Merkl and his girl-friend Erna*)
FRANZ MERKL Parlez-vous française?
CASIMIR No.
FRANZ MERKL Pity.
CASIMIR Why?
FRANZ MERKL Because you can't say it in German. A quotation. Regarding the roller-coaster and Caroline — (*to Erna*) if you did that to me, I'd beat you black and blue.
ERNA You're so unfair.

SCENE 11

CAROLINE (*on the roller-coaster, shrieks as it whizzes down*)
CASIMIR (*staring up at it*) Have a safe ride, Missie. I just hope nothing happens to you — like breaking your neck.
FRANZ MERKL You've no need to worry, we're together in this.
CASIMIR I'm not together in this. I don't want to be together in this. I'm alone.
(*silence*)
FRANZ MERKL I've got a better suggestion. Leave the man alone —— it's not his fault your girl's up there whizzing through the stratosphere. It's her your quarrel's with. Just bawl the hell out of her the moment she appears.
CASIMIR That's a matter of opinion.
FRANZ MERKL Of course.
(*silence*)
CASIMIR But that's not my opinion.
FRANZ MERKL You're naive, that's all.
CASIMIR Probably.
(*silence*)
FRANZ MERKL What are women? Do you know the one about the girl with her own father and brother ——
ERNA (*interrupts him*) You shouldn't talk like that about us women, running us down all the time.

(*silence*)
FRANZ MERKL How would you like me to talk about them?
ERNA I'm a woman too, you know.
FRANZ MERKL Keep your hair on! Here, hold my gloves for me, I need to go and get something to cheer me up — (*exit; a French horn is heard in the distance, playing a melancholy tune*)

SCENE 12

ERNA Casimir. Look up there. The Big Dipper.
CASIMIR Where?
ERNA There. And that there's Orion. With his sword.
CASIMIR How do you know all that?
ERNA My employer explained it all to me when I was still in service — he was a professor. You know, when things aren't going too well, I always think to myself, what's a person compared with a star. It gives me something to hold on to.

SCENE 13

SCHÜRZINGER (*enters; the French horn stops*)
CASIMIR (*recognizes him*)
SCHÜRZINGER (*nods*)
CASIMIR (*nods back, automatically*)
SCHÜRZINGER Your fiancée's still on the roller-coaster.
CASIMIR (*giving him and angry look*) Great!

SCENE 14

FRANZ MERKL (*reappears; he has bought two pairs of wieners which he proceeds to tuck into with every sign of enjoyment*)

SCENE 15

SCHÜRZINGER I only had one ride. Your fiancée's having another go.
CASIMIR Another go.
SCHÜRZINGER Sure.
(*silence*)
CASIMIR Sure. So, you're an old friend of my fiancée's?
SCHÜRZINGER What do you mean?
CASIMIR What do you mean, what do you mean?
SCHÜRZINGER No, there must be some mistake. I only met your finacée just now, by the ice-cream van — we just happened to get talking.
CASIMIR Just happened —
SCHÜRZINGER Oh definitely.
CASIMIR That's all I needed.
SCHÜRZINGER Why do you say that?
CASIMIR It's very odd. You see, my finacée told me she'd known you for a long time. For ages, she said.
FRANZ MERKL Emgoddambarrassing.
(*silence*)
SCHÜRZINGER I'm terribly sorry about all this,
CASIMIR But is it true or is it not true? I'd like to get this clear. Man to man.
(*silence*)
SCHÜRZINGER No. It's not true.
CASIMIR Cross your heart?
SCHÜRZINGER Cross my heart.
CASIMIR OK. Thanks.
(*silence*)
FRANZ MERKL You're not going to get anywhere like this, Casimir. Sock him one —
CASIMIR You keep out of this, please.
FRANZ MERKL Oh, just listen to him! Wimp!
CASIMIR I'm not a wimp.
FRANZ MERKL You'll find out where these pussyfooting methods get you soon enough. I can already see you licking the ass of your

fiancée's fancy man. Oh yes, you worship the ground she treads on! Next thing you'll be getting a thrill out of going down on your bended knees to kiss her sweaty feet, you masochist!
CASIMIR I'm not a masochist. I'm straight.
(*silence*)
FRANZ MERKL That's the thanks you get. I try to help you and you start getting personal. I should just go and leave you to it.
ERNA Come on, Franz.
FRANZ MERKL (*pinches her on the arm*)
ERNA Ouch! Ouch!
FRANZ MERKL I don't care how much you squawk, I'm staying here as long as I like. A man doesn't leave his friend in the lurch in a situation like this.

SCENE 16

CAROLINE (*enters*)
(*silence*)

SCENE 17

CASIMIR (*slowly goes up to Caroline and stops close in front of her*) Earlier on I asked you what I was to understand by your saying that we two might perhaps no longer be meant for each other. And you said, "Perhaps." That's what you said.
CAROLINE And you said I was leaving you because you'd lost your job. That's very insulting. Any self-respecting woman would stick by her man more than ever if he's on hard times.
CASIMIR And you're a self-respecting woman?
CAROLINE You're the one who can answer that.
CASIMIR And you're sticking by me more than ever now?
CAROLINE (*says nothing*)
CASIMIR You have to give me an answer.
CAROLINE I can't give you an answer to that, not if you don't feel it.

(*silence*)
CASIMIR Why have you been lying?
CAROLINE I haven't been lying.
CASIMIR Yes you have, lying quite shamelessly.
(*silence*)
CAROLINE And when did I do that?
CASIMIR Earlier on. You said you'd known this man for ages. For ages, those were your words. And he's just someone you met at the Oktoberfest. Why did you lie to me?
(*silence*)
CAROLINE I was very angry.
CASIMIR That's no reason.
CAROLINE It is for a woman perhaps.
CASIMIR No.
(*silence*)
CAROLINE I just wanted to have an ice-cream, but then we got talking about the Zeppelin. You're not usually so petty.
CASIMIR I can't put all this behind me just like that.
CAROLINE But I just wanted to have a ride on the roller-coaster.
(*silence*)
CASIMIR If you'd said, Casimir darling, I'm just dying to have a ride on the roller-coaster, then I'd have said, Off you go and have your ride.
CAROLINE Oh, don't come the perfect cavalier with me!
CASIMIR Go on, get it off your chest. — Who's that anyway?
CAROLINE A gentleman. He's a tailor's cutter.
(*silence*)
CASIMIR So you think a tailor's cutter's a gentleman and an honest chauffeur's not?
CAROLINE Why do you always have to twist everything I say?
CASIMIR I leave that to you. I'm just establishing the facts, and the facts are that you lied to me without good reason. Why don't you just buzz off with your tailor's cutter!? Of course he's a real gentlemen, not like some poor bastard who's just lost his job.
CAROLINE And do I have to go round with a long face just because you've lost your job. You can't stand seeing someone else enjoying themselves! You're so selfish!

CASIMIR Since when have I been selfish? Don't make me laugh! This isn't about your roller-coaster ride, this is about your impossible behavior in lying to me.
SCHÜRZINGER Excuse me —
FRANZ MERKL (*interrupts him*) You just shut up and get the hell out of here. Fuck off, I tell you!
CASIMIR Leave him alone, Franz. They make a perfect pair. (*to Caroline*) Tailor's whore!
(*silence*)
CAROLINE What did you just say?
FRANZ MERKL He just said "tailor's whore." Or tart, if you prefer.
SCHÜRZINGER (*to Caroline*) Come on, I think we'd better go.
CAROLINE Yes, I'm coming — (*leaves with Schürzinger*)

SCENE 18

FRANZ MERKL (*watches them leave*) Bon voyage!
CASIMIR Together!
FRANZ MERKL Women are two a penny. (*to Erna*) Two a penny!
ERNA Why do you have to be so nasty? What have I done to you?
FRANZ MERKL You're just another woman. Right, now Franz Merkl's going to buy himself a beer. To cheer himself up. You come along too, Casimir.
CASIMIR No. I'm off home. I'm going to bed. (*exit*)

SCENE 19

FRANZ MERKL (*shouting after him*) Good night.

SCENE 20

The orchestra plays Leon Jessel's "Parade of the Tin Soldiers."

SCENE 21

At the bottom of the chute-the-chutes.
The people slide down the chute on their backsides and if the men watching at the bottom are lucky they get a squint up the women's skirts. Rauch and Speer are among those watching.
On the left is an ice-cream vendor who also sells Turkish delight and balloons; on the right a fried-chicken stand which is not doing much business because most people can't afford it.
Maria and Elli slide down the chute-the-chutes; you can see up their skirts.
The air is full of fairground music.

SCENE 22

RAUCH (*winks at Elli and Maria who are adjusting their brassieres, which have slipped during the slide*)

ELLI Look at that dirty old man.
MARIA Geriatric!
ELLI A real horny old goat!
MARIA I think the other's from the North.
ELLI How come you say that?
RAUCH (*still grinning*)
ELLI (*gives him a friendly smile, but speaks so he can't hear*) Filthy pimp.
RAUCH (*flattered, gives her a little bow*)
ELLI (*as above*) Good evening, pisspot.
RAUCH (*slobbering at the lips*)
ELLI (*as above*) You'd just love that, wouldn't you, you old shithouse. You should be thinking about death rather than the opposite. (*exit with Maria, laughing uproariously*)

SCENE 23

RAUCH We're on our way!
SPEER Pretty as sin, what?
RAUCH Despite all the crises, it's still the same old Oktoberfest. The Chancellor can't kill it off however much he talks about austerity. Do I exaggerate?
SPEER Just like the good old days.
RAUCH You get a porter sitting next to a counsellor, a businessman next to a tradesman, a minister next to a laborer — that's what I call democracy. (*goes with Speer to the fried-chicken stand; they eat a tender, crispy chicken and drink kirsch and beer*)

SCENE 24

CAROLINE (*enters with Schürzinger; she is a little in front of him and suddenly stops, so he does too*) Do men always have to be suspicious? We do everything they want as it is.
SCHÜRZINGER Of course, as a man you have to have yourself under control. — You mustn't get me wrong.
CAROLINE How do you mean?
SCHÜRZINGER Because I was sticking up for your fiancé just now. He's pretty cut up. After all, it's not easy, suddenly finding yourself out of a job.
CAROLINE Sure. But that's no reason for him to call me a whore. You have to be able to keep things separate, the economic crisis and private matters.
SCHÜRZINGER But in my opinion the public domain and the private sphere are inextricably interwoven.
CAROLINE Just listen to the professor! Can't you talk like a normal person? I'm having another ice-cream. (*she buys one from the ice-cream vendor; Schürzinger gets another cornet to lick as well*)

SCENE 25

RAUCH (*pointing at Caroline as he eats his chicken*) Nice ass that girl's got —
SPEER Very nice.
RAUCH Without an ass a girl's not a real girl.
SPEER Very true.

SCENE 26

SCHÜRZINGER All I'm saying is that if you're going to split up you should think about it carefully and consider the consequences.
CAROLINE Consequences? What consequences? I've a job of my own.
SCHÜRZINGER It was the psychological aspects I had in mind.
(*silence*)
CAROLINE It's not in my nature to let someone insult me like that. I've been a fool to commit myself body and soul to that Casimir — I've already thrown up two chances of marrying men with state jobs and a guaranteed pension.
(*silence*)
SCHÜRZINGER It's just that I'd be unhappy if it happened to look as if I were to blame for the estrangement between you and him. — A man and a woman split up because of me once before. Never again!
CAROLINE Back there you said when a man loses his job his girl starts to fall out of love with him. It's automatic, you said.
SCHÜRZINGER It's just the way we are. Unfortunately.
CAROLINE What's your first name?
SCHÜRZINGER Eugene.
CAROLINE You've got striking eyes.
SCHÜRZINGER I've been told that before.
CAROLINE Don't let it go to your head.
(*silence*)
SCHÜRZINGER Do you like Eugene as a name?
CAROLINE I might get to like it.

(*silence*)
SCHÜRZINGER I'm a lonely man, you know. My mother, for example, she's been deaf since the inflation, and not quite right in the head, either, because she lost everything. — I haven't got a living soul I can have a heart-to-heart with.
CAROLINE You've no brothers or sisters?
SCHÜRZINGER No. I'm an only child.
CAROLINE Come on, I can't take any more ice-cream. (*exit with Schürzinger*)

SCENE 27

SPEER Strange these young people of today. We did a lot of sport too, of course, but to show so little appreciation of the finer things in life —
RAUCH Not a sensual generation at all.
SPEER (*with a grin*) At least that means they avoid some things.
RAUCH I've always been lucky.
SPEER Me too. Except once.
RAUCH Was she pretty at least?
SPEER You don't look at the mantelpiece when you're poking the fire.
RAUCH (*raising his glass*) Your very good health.

SCENE 28

CAROLINE (*slides down the chute followed by Schürzinger; Rauch and Speer get a look up her skirt*).
SCHÜRZINGER (*sees Rauch, starts then raises his hat to him very politely, raises it twice even*)

SCENE 29

RAUCH (*surprised, nods back; to Speer*) Who can that be? That man with the girl with the nice ass's just raised his hat to me —

SCENE 30

CAROLINE (*fiddling with her brassiere like the other girls*) Who's that there?
SCHÜRZINGER Him. Mr. Rauch. My boss. You know the big firm, four stories and an extension at the back?
CAROLINE Oh yes.
SCHÜRZINGER He made himself into an Inc. last June, but that was only for appearances and for tax and all that.

SCENE 31

RAUCH (*has arranged something with Speer and now comes up to Schürzinger; he is already slightly tipsy*) Excuse me, have we met somewhere?
SCHÜRZINGER My name's Schürzinger, Mr. Rauch, sir.
RAUCH Schürzinger?
SCHÜRZINGER Children's clothes. Children's coats section. (*silence*)
RAUCH (*to Schürzinger*) Your fiancée?
CAROLINE No.
RAUCH (*pops a cigar into Schürzinger's mouth*) Nice to see you. (*to Caroline*) Would you allow a fat capitalist to offer you a kirsch?
CAROLINE No thanks. Kirsch doesn't agree with me. You can buy me some of that sweet Greek wine though.
RAUCH A Samos it is, then. (*goes over to the fried chicken stand*) A Samos for the young lady. (*to Caroline*) This is my best friend, he's a northerner, from Erfurt in Thuringia. And I'm from Weiden,

that's north of here too, but still in Bavaria. And a kirsch for this young man here.
SCHÜRZINGER I'm sorry, Mr.Rauch., sir, but I never drink alcohol.

SCENE 32

CASIMIR (*enters and observes*)

SCENE 33

RAUCH Why ever not?
SCHÜRZINGER I'm a teetotaler, Mr. Rauch sir.
SPEER On principle?
SCHÜRZINGER You could put it like that.
RAUCH Well we don't recognize those principles here. We delete them from the statute book. Surely a young man like you won't refuse to have a kirsch with his Lordandmaster. Down the hatch, Mr. er —
SCHÜRZINGER Schürzinger. (*empties the glass with a grimace*)
RAUCH Schürzinger! I had a schoolteacher called Schürzinger. He was a real rhinoceros. Another glass of Samos. And another kirsch for our young teetotaler. He's just lost his virginity as far as alcohol's concerned. You too, young lady?
CAROLINE Certainly not! I just don't drink spirits, and I don't like mixed stuff at all — (*sees Casimir*)

SCENE 34

CASIMIR (*waves her over*)
CAROLINE (*ignores him*)
CASIMIR (*waves more emphatically*)
CAROLINE (*empties her glass; irritated, she deliberately takes her time putting it down then goes slowly over to Casimir*)

SCENE 35

RAUCH Who's that? Don Quixote?
SCHÜRZINGER That's the young lady's fiancé.
SPEER Big scene coming up!
SCHÜRZINGER But she doesn't want anything to do with him anymore.
RAUCH That's what I like to hear.

SCENE 36

CAROLINE What do you want now?
(*silence*)
CASIMIR Who're they?
CAROLINE Just some people I've known for ages.
CASIMIR There's no need to be sarcastic.
CAROLINE I'm not being sarcastic. The fat one there's Mr. Rauch. He owns the clothing factory. Sole owner. The other comes from the North. He's president of a district court.
CASIMIR Oh, a couple of toffs. I'm not going to get sore at you anymore.
(*silence*)
CAROLINE What is it you want?
CASIMIR I wanted to ask you to forgive me for being so suspicious just now and for talking to you like that. That wasn't very nice. Can you forgive me?
CAROLINE Yes.
CASIMIR Thank you. I feel better now — (*smiles*)
CAROLINE You don't appreciate the situation.
CASIMIR What situation?
(*silence*)
CAROLINE There's no point, Casimir. I've thought it over, I've searched my heart, and — (*turns back towards the fried-chicken stand*)
CASIMIR But you don't want to have anything to do with them! They'll just use you for their own pleasure.

CAROLINE Don't be so sentimental. Life's tough and a woman who wants to get anywhere has to use her charms to attract an influential man.
CASIMIR Is that what you did to me?
CAROLINE Yes.
(*silence*)
CASIMIR That's not true.
CAROLINE Oh yes it is.
(*silence*)
CASIMIR And where do you think you're going to get with those two gentlemen there?
CAROLINE One step up the social ladder perhaps.
CASIMIR That's a new attitude for you.
CAROLINE No, it's not a new attitude. I let you dictate to me. I followed you in pretending an office girl was just another proletarian. But in here (*points to her heart*) I always knew different. My heart and my mind were blinded because I'd become dependent on you. But that's over now.
CASIMIR Over?
CAROLINE You said it.
(*silence*)
CASIMIR Oh. So that's the way it is, is it? Casimir's been dismissed. They're all the same. No exceptions.
CAROLINE Is there anything else you want to say to me?
(*silence*)
CASIMIR I spent ages going round and round wondering if I should ask you to forgive me — a complete waste of time. (*exit*)

SCENE 37

CAROLINE (*watches him go and then turns back to the stand*)
(*dark*)

SCENE 38

The orchestra plays "The Last Rose of Summer."

SCENE 39

In the freak show. The auditorium is crammed full of people, Rauch, Speer, Caroline and Schürzinger among them

SCENE 40

MC Our fifth exhibit is the Man with the Head of a Bulldog!
THE MAN WITH THE HEAD OF A BULLDOG *(comes onto the stage)*
MC John, the Man with the Head of a Bulldog, was sixteen yesterday. As you can see the lower jaw is abnormally well developed so that he can easily cover his nose with his lower lip.
THE MAN WITH THE HEAD OF A BULLDOG *(does so)*
MC John cannot open his mouth, so he has to be fed artificially. He could have an extremely tricky operation to allow him to open his mouth, but then he wouldn't be able to close it at all. Here you can see the tricks nature sometimes plays and the strange people there are in the world.
THE MAN WITH THE HEAD OF A BULLDOG *(bows and goes off)*

SCENE 41

MC And now, ladies and gentlemen, our sixth exhibit and the highlight of our show, Juanita the Gorilla Girl!
JUANITA *(comes on stage)*
MC Juanita was born in a little village near Zwickau. Why her physical development was not the same as that of normal children is one of the mysteries of modern science. As you can see for yourselves, ladies and gentlemen, Juanita's body is covered all

over with animal fur. The arrangement of her internal organs also resembles that of an animal —

SCENE 42

A whirring noise, getting louder and louder, screams outside and a fanfare from the orchestra

RAUCH (*jumps up from his seat*) The Zeppelin! The Zeppelin! (*The noise is deafening; the audience rushes outside to see the Zeppelin doing its loops over the Oktoberfest.*)

SCENE 43

JUANITA (*wants to go out as well*)
MC Are you mad?! Get back inside!
JUANITA But the Zeppelin —
MC Out of the question. Impossible. Get back.

SCENE 44

THE MAN WITH THE HEAD OF A BULLDOG (*appears with the other freaks, the Fat Lady, the Giant, the Bearded Girl, the Camel-Man and the Siamese Twins*)
MC Who called you lot?! What do you think you're doing?
THE FAT LADY But the Zeppelin —

SCENE 45

THE MIDGET (*appears with a whip*) Henry, what's going on here?
MC These cripples are going crazy boss! They want to see the Zeppelin.
MIDGET (*sharply*) Anyone got anything to say?

(*silence*)
MIDGET Back to your places. And look quick about it! Want to see the Zeppelin! If people see you outside we're ruined. A load of commies, that's what you are.
JUANITA I won't be talked to like that. (*bursts into tears*)
THE MAN WITH THE HEAD OF A BULLDOG (*wheezes, staggers and clutches his chest*)
THE FAT LADY John! John!
MIDGET Off you go! At the double!
THE FAT LADY (*supporting the Man with the Head of a Bulldog*) Poor John! He's got such a weak heart. (*goes off with the other freaks; only Juanita stays*)

SCENE 46

MIDGET (*suddenly gentle*) Come on Juanita, my little girl, there's no need to cry — here's some candy for you — lovely chocolates.
JUANITA You shouldn't keep on calling me names, it's a very unchristian thing to do.
MIDGET No offense meant. There you are — (*gives her the whole box of candy and exits*)

SCENE 47

JUANITA (*eats the candy listlessly; in the meantime Caroline and Schürzinger come back into the auditorium and sit down in the back row*)

SCENE 48

CAROLINE It looks lovely, the Zeppelin — even in the dark, with all those lights. But we're never going to go in it.
SCHÜRZINGER No, we're not.
CAROLINE Why are you looking at me in that funny way?.

SCHÜRZINGER Why are you?
(*silence*)
CAROLINE I think I must be a little bit drunk. And you've never had alcohol before?
SCHÜRZINGER No, never.
CAROLINE Are you as abstemious in other things?
SCHÜRZINGER I wouldn't go so far as to say that.
CAROLINE (*suddenly gives him a quick kiss*)
(*silence*)
SCHÜRZINGER I really don't know whether I'm coming or going. Is it the alcohol or — there's something going on inside me I can't control. If we had money, for example —
CAROLINE (*interrupts him*) Oh, come on, Eugene, don't be such a bore!
SCHÜRZINGER Eugene? We're on first-name terms now, are we?
CAROLINE For this evening —
SCHÜRZINGER And after that?
CAROLINE We'll see.
(*silence*)

SCENE 49

RAUCH (*comes back into the booth, sees Caroline and Schürzinger, stops by the entrance and listens*)
CAROLINE Your name is Eugene?
SCHÜRZINGER Yes.
CAROLINE And mine's Caroline. Why are you laughing?
SCHÜRZINGER Because I'm happy.
RAUCH And I'm Conrad.
SCHÜRZINGER (*starts; Caroline too*)
(*silence*)
SCHÜRZINGER (*stands up*)
RAUCH (*grins and wags his finger at them*) Now then, naughty little Caroline. Who's sitting in here while the Zeppelin's flying round outside?

CAROLINE The Zeppelin, the Zeppelin. I've had enough of the Zeppelin.
(*silence*)
RAUCH (*gives Schürzinger an irritated glare*) Congratulations.
SCHÜRZINGER (*bows, embarrassed*)
RAUCH (*angrily*) Don't mind me, you just carry on with your animated conversation —
SCHÜRZINGER Animated, Mr. Rauch, sir? Oh, animated's quite different, you know— (*smiles politely and sits down*)
RAUCH Different?

SCENE 50

SPEER (*has followed Rauch in*) What an odious guy.
RAUCH A cynic.
SPEER All over poor little Carrie while we're outside watching the Zepp.
RAUCH It'll soon be all over for him.

SCENE 51

The orchestra quietly starts to play the "Radetzky March" and the audience comes back into the booth now the Zeppelin's on its way back to Friedrichshafen. When everyone is seated again the orchestra breaks off in the middle of a bar.

SCENE 52

CAROLINE What do you mean by saying you aren't animated?
SCHÜRZINGER That was just a tactical move.
CAROLINE I can hear you moving away already. You're very calculating. Does that go for love too?
SCHÜRZINGER No, what you're thinking's a total misunderstanding.

CAROLINE I'm not thinking, I'm just saying.

SCENE 53

MC (*strikes the gong*) Ladies and gentlemen, where had we got to? Juanita, as I told you, is covered all over in animal fur and the arrangement of her internal organs resembles that of an animal. And yet she has an extremely vivid imagination. She can speak perfect English and French, both of which she taught herself by dint of determination and hard work. And now, ladies and gentlemen, with your permission Juanita will delight you with her natural soprano. Music, maestro, please — (*Someone plays the barcarole from the "Tales of Hoffmann" on an out-of-tune piano.*)

SCENE 54

JUANITA (*sings, and while she sings Schürzinger puts his arm round Caroline's waist and her calf and his shin come into contact*)
Lovely night, o night of love,
With promise of fulfillment.
Moon and stars shine from above
Upon our night of love.
Time stands still, we feel the thrill of hearts united in passion,
Here in this secluded spot so far from the rush of time.
The soft caressing breeze
Sighs of love in the branches.
O soft caressing breeze
Cool our cheeks with your kiss.

160 *Casimir and Caroline*

SCENE 55

The curtain falls before the end of the verse. Now that Juanita has finished her song, the midget crosses the stage in front of the curtain from left to right, holding a sign saying "Intermission."

SCENE 56

Intermission.

SCENE 57

The audience lights go down in the booth and the orchestra plays Adolph Scherzer's "Bavarian March-Past." The curtain rises again.

SCENE 58

In the Wagnerbräu tent, with its brass band. Franz Merkl is in an expansive mood, his girl-friend Erna somewhat restrained, while Casimir is hunched up next to them, the picture of melancholy.

SCENE 59

ALL (*apart from Casimir join in with the brass band*)
As long as old St Peter's
Stands on St Peter's hill,
As long as Isar's waters
Flow green through Munich still,
As long as on the Platzl
The Hofbräuhaus serves beer
The citizens of Munich
will ever be of good cheer,

The citizens of Munich
Will ever be of good cheer.
ending in a general toast
So here's to, so cheers to good old Munich beer
So here's to, so cheers to good old Munich beer.
One, two, three — down the hatch.

SCENE 60

FRANZ MERKL Cheers, Casimir. Get something down you or you'll never get anywhere.
CASIMIR Oh yes, where am I going to get? The president's seat in the board room?
FRANZ MERKL Well start up a new party and make yourself minister of finance.
CASIMIR Go on, kick a man when he's down.
FRANZ MERKL Some people just won't listen.
(*silence*)
CASIMIR I've got my driver's license and I'm a driver.
FRANZ MERKL Just be glad you haven't got your fiancée anymore. Arrogant bitch!
CASIMIR The young lady works in an office.
FRANZ MERKL That's no excuse.
CASIMIR All women are inferior beings — present company excepted, of course. They sell their souls and betray their men, in this particular case me for a roller-coaster.
ERNA If I was a man I wouldn't touch a woman. The smell alone — especially in winter.

SCENE 61

ALL (*apart from Casimir, join in with the brass band*)
In forest wild I shoot the stag,
The hind in woody brake,
The eagle on its rocky crag

The duck upon the lake.
No glen, no rocky cliff can hide
Them when my shot rings out,
Yet I, a huntsman steely-eyed,
Still feel the pangs of love.
(*sudden silence*)

SCENE 62

CASIMIR Yet I a huntsman steely-eyed, still feel the pangs of love — and love is a shining star that turns the humblest cottage into a gilded palace — and love never ends —— as long as you don't lose your job, that is. All these ideals of the spiritual union of two people!? Adam and Eve! I don't give a shit for it — My total assets are four marks, but tonight I'm going to get drunk then hang myself — and tomorrow people will say, Remember that poor guy called Casimir —
FRANZ MERKL The people'll say fuck all. There's thousands die every day — and they're forgotten even before they die. Perhaps if you were a politician and died you'd be buried with pomp and circumstance and then be forgotten tomorrow — forgotten!
CASIMIR Yes, we're pretty much on our own in this world.
FRANZ MERKL Here's mud in your eye, asshole!

SCENE 63

ALL (*apart from Casimir, join in with the band again*)
Drink, drink, lift up your glass,
Leave all your worries at home.
Drink, drink, lift up your glass,
Leave all your worries at home.
Leave your trouble and leave your care —
You'll soon be walking on air.
Leave your trouble and leave your care
And you'll soon be walking on air.
(*sudden silence*)

SCENE 64

CASIMIR (*standing up*) Right. It's time I got down to basics. What I really ought to do is go round to Caroline's place, pull all the clothes out of her closet and tear them to rags. Now people are going to see how nasty I can be! (*staggers off*)

SCENE 65

ERNA Where's he off to?
FRANZ MERKL He'll be back, as long as he doesn't flush himself down the pan.
ERNA I'm really worried —
FRANZ MERKL He won't do anything silly.
ERNA I don't think he's a very robust type. He's sensitive rather.
FRANZ MERKL That's very observant of you.
(*silence*)
ERNA Franz — let him go. Please.
FRANZ MERKL Who?
ERNA Casimir.
FRANZ MERKL What d'you mean, let him go.
ERNA He doesn't belong with us, I can feel it. — Please don't try to push him into anything.
FRANZ MERKL And why not, might I ask?
ERNA Because the things we do are — nothing.
FRANZ MERKL Since when?
(*silence*)
ERNA Hey, take your fingers out of my beer.
FRANZ MERKL That's very observant of you.
ERNA Get your fingers out —
FRANZ MERKL No. It cools me down. I'm so hot-blooded.
ERNA (*suddenly yanks his fingers out of her beer glass*)
FRANZ MERKL (*gives a baffled grin*)

SCENE 66

ALL (*apart from Erna and Franz Merkl, join in with the band again. Rauch, Speer, Caroline and Schürzinger walk past, quart beer glasses in their hands, paper hats on their heads and carrying novelty items. They are also joining in the singing, of course.*)
Drink, drink, lift up your glass,
Leave all your worries at home.
Drink, drink, lift up your glass,
Leave all your worries at home.
Leave your trouble and leave your care —
You'll soon be walking on air.
Leave your trouble and leave your care
And you'll soon be walking on air.
(*sudden silence*)

SCENE 67

CASIMIR (*enters with Elli and Maria; he has his arms round both of them*) Meet my friends. We three beautiful people met outside the toilets. It's an unexplained mystery why the ladies always have to go to the rest room in pairs. Can you explain it, Franz?
MARIA Now then!
FRANZ MERKL No nowthenning here, my girl.
CASIMIR We're all only human, especially tonight. (*sits down and gets Elli to sit on his lap*)
ELLI (*to Franz Merkl, with a nod in Casimir's direction*) Is it true he's got a big motor?
FRANZ MERKL Of course he's got a big motor. You should just see it!
MARIA (*to Elli*) Don't you listen to them, they're just putting you on. Where'd he get a motor from?
CASIMIR (*to Maria*) If I say I've got a big motor, then I've got a big motor, just get that into your thick skull.
ELLI Hey, lay off, Maria.
CASIMIR (*caressing Elli*) You're okay, you're my kind of girl. You've got lovely soft hair and smooth skin.
ELLI I'd like a drink.

CASIMIR There you are. Get that down you.
ELLI There's nothing left in it.
CASIMIR Beer! Over here!
WAITRESS (*puts a glass on the table as she passes*) I'll take the money for that now, please.
CASIMIR (*going through his pockets*) Money, money, money — Jesus, is that all my money gone already —
WAITRESS (*takes the glass away again*)
ELLI (*stands up*)
MARIA A big motor? Him? I said right off he'd have a bicycle at most. On the installment plan!
CASIMIR (*to Elli*) Oh come on —
ELLI (*waving goodbye*) So long, Mr. Big Motor — (*exit with Maria*)

SCENE 68

CASIMIR Money, money — without money, Casimir my old friend, you're the lowest of the low.
FRANZ MERKL Casimir the philosopher.
CASIMIR If I only knew which party I should vote for —
FRANZ MERKL Casimir the politician.
CASIMIR You can kiss my ass, Merkl!
(*silence*)
FRANZ MERKL Look at me.
CASIMIR (*looks at him*)
FRANZ MERKL Apart from the odd splinter group, there's no political party I haven't joined at some time or other. And everywhere it's the decent people who're taken for suckers. When society's in the state it is the only answer is to do what a certain Franz Merkl does.
CASIMIR And that is?
FRANZ MERKL Simple.
(*silence*)
FRANZ MERKL For example I've been specializing lately in certain — aspects of the law.

CASIMIR I don't want to get involved with the law.
FRANZ MERKL You lunkhead! (*waves a ten-mark note under his nose*)
(*silence*)
CASIMIR No. There's not much point in that kind of private operation.
ERNA Caroline's sitting over there.
CASIMIR (*standing up*) Where?
(*silence*)
FRANZ MERKL She's seen you.
CASIMIR But she's not coming over.
(*silence*)

SCENE 69

CASIMIR (*makes a speech to the far-off Caroline*) My dear Caroline, you don't have to come over here, our relations are over, and that goes for human relations as well. You can't help it. If I lose my job, then it's quite natural, you slut, you floozy. But if I teamed up with Franz Merkl now, that would be your fault and yours alone — because there's nothing left inside me. That's where you used to be, inside me, but today you moved out — leaving me like a reed in the wind with nothing to hold on to. — (*sits down*)

SCENE 70

(*silence*)
FRANZ MERKL Well?
CASIMIR All that's left is an aching void.
FRANZ MERKL For the last time, Casimir, what about my offer? You can't help someone who won't help themselves.
CASIMIR I can't say yet.
FRANZ MERKL (*holding out his hand to Casimir*) It's in your own hand —
CASIMIR (*staring absently into space*) I can't say yet.

ERNA Leave him alone if he doesn't want to.
(*silence*)
FRANZ MERKL (*stares at Erna angrily — suddenly throws his beer in her face*)
ERNA (*jumps up*)
FRANZ MERKL (*pushes her back down in her seat*) You stay there! The next time it'll be my foot in your face.

SCENE 71

ALL (*apart from Casimir, Erna and Franz Merkl, sing*)
And when the roses blossom
We know winter is gone.
But the roses of Maytime
Flow'r for us once alone.
All the birds leave in autumn
And fly back with the sun,
But once we have departed,
We will never return.
(*dark*)

SCENE 72

The orchestra plays the "St. Petersburg Sleigh Ride" by Richard Eilenberg.

SCENE 73

At the entrance to the tent with the horse rides. Rauch, Speer, Caroline and Schürzinger enter

SCENE 74

RAUCH (*to Caroline*) How about a dashing ride? This is the hippodrome!
CAROLINE Great! But no sidesaddle — that way you get a better grip.
RAUCH Attagirl!
SPEER Spoken like a true horsewoman.
CAROLINE When I have a ride I always want two goes.
RAUCH Have three if you like.
CAROLINE Great! (*goes off into the ring*)

SCENE 75

SPEER (*calls out to her as she goes*) Four if you like.
RAUCH Umpteen! (*goes up onto the raised platform with Speer and orders a bottle of wine*)
SCHÜRZINGER (*stays down at the bottom and stares at Caroline all the time. An old lame horse with a shortsighted ten-year-old girl sitting sidesaddle on it is led past the platform into the ring — some music immediately starts up and keeps breaking off in the middle of a bar, when a certain number of turns round the arena have been completed and another payment is due; the crack of riding whips can be heard. Schürzinger stands on a chair to get a better view; Rauch and Speer are also watching, of course*)

SCENE 76

RAUCH Look at that! What a girl!
SPEER A real horsewoman!
RAUCH A natural! Just look at the way those boobs wobble! Seen from behind, girls on bikes remind me of ducks swimming.
SPEER (*pours himself more wine*) Christ, Rauch, it's ages since I had a horse between my legs!
RAUCH Really?

SPEER 1912. I could afford to keep two horses then. Nowadays? A poor judge like me?! Those were the days. Two Arab mares. Rosalind and Yvonne.
RAUCH (*picks up his wine glass as well*) You married late in life as well, didn't you?
SPEER Still early enough.
RAUCH Goes without saying. (*raises his glass*) Your very good health!
(*silence*)
RAUCH I sent my wife to Arosa and any number of health resorts — the boy's as fit as a fiddle.
SPEER When does he graduate?
RAUCH Next semester. We're getting old.
(*silence*)
SPEER I've got two grandchildren already. There's always a part of you lives on. A few atoms.

SCENE 77

CAROLINE (*reappears and ignores Schürzinger as she walks past him; he is still standing on his chair*)
SCHÜRZINGER (*in a low voice*) Hey, wait a minute! Just a friendly warning.
CAROLINE Oh dear!
SCHÜRZINGER What do you mean, "Oh dear"?
CAROLINE When a man says that he's got an ulterior motive.
SCHÜRZINGER (*slowly gets down off the chair and goes up close to Caroline*) I haven't got any ulterior motive. I've just sobered up a little. Don't drink any more alcohol. Please.
CAROLINE No. Today I'm going to drink as much as I want.
SCHÜRZINGER You couldn't imagine what those two gentlemen over there are saying about you.
CAROLINE And what are they saying about me?
SCHÜRZINGER They'd like to get you drunk.
CAROLINE Oh, I can hold my drink.
(*silence*)

SCHÜRZINGER And my boss, Mr. Rauch, he's quite open about it.
CAROLINE About what?
SCHÜRZINGER That he'd like to have you. Sexually. Tonight.
(*silence*)
CAROLINE He would, would he. Like to have me —
SCHÜRZINGER He says it in front of me as if I were thin air. You shouldn't be going round with people like that. They're beneath you. Come on, let's slip away —
CAROLINE Where to?
(*silence*)
SCHÜRZINGER We can have a cup of tea together. At my place perhaps.
(*silence*)
CAROLINE You're only thinking of yourself, too. A real Casimir.
SCHÜRZINGER You've lost me there.
CAROLINE Yes, Casimir.
SCHÜRZINGER My name's Eugene.
CAROLINE And mine's Caroline.
(*silence*)
SCHÜRZINGER I'm very shy you know, but just now, in the freak show, I was dreaming of a future together. But that was just Lady Caroline indulging in a passing fancy.
CAROLINE Yes, Lord Eugene.
SCHÜRZINGER You often waste your emotions —
CAROLINE If you have no emotions you have a much easier time of it. (*walks off, leaving him standing, and goes over to the platform; Schürzinger sits down on the chair*)

SCENE 78

RAUCH Congratulations!
SPEER I can tell you've got a talent for it, and I should know, I was in the cavalry.
CAROLINE I thought you were a judge.
SPEER Have you ever come across a judge in Germany who hadn't been an officer in the army? I haven't.

RAUCH There are a few —
SPEER All Jews!
CAROLINE No politics, please.
SPEER But that's not politics.
RAUCH Politics — yuck! (*raises his glass to Caroline*) To our next ride.
CAROLINE I'd really love to have another ride. The three goes went so quickly.
RAUCH Three more then!
SPEER (*raises his glass*) To Rosalind and Yvonne. Where are you now? You're still with me in spirit. What's a convertible compared to a horse?
CAROLINE Oh, a convertible's definitely got class.
SPEER (*in a melancholy tone*) But you haven't got living flesh between your knees —
RAUCH (*softly*) I've got a very classy convertible, as I'm sure you won't mind me mentioning. I hope you'll come for a ride?
(*silence*)
CAROLINE Where to?
RAUCH To Altötting. Where they go on pilgrimage.
CAROLINE To Altötting, okay — (*goes back into the riding arena; on the way she passes Schürzinger who is examining his blackheads in a pocket mirror*)

SCENE 79

RAUCH (*already rather drunk; he is blithely waving his arms, as if he were the conductor of the hippodrome orchestra, which is playing a waltz*)
SPEER (*even more drunk*) Altötting? Where's Altötting?
RAUCH (*singing to the waltz*) Up in my — penthouse flat — one two three — between my — silken sheets — one two three — (*hums*)
SPEER (*bitchily*) And your employee over there?
(*The music breaks off in the middle of a bar.*)
RAUCH (*slaps the table and glares at Speer*)

172 *Casimir and Caroline*

(*The music starts up again, with a march, "In the Gypsy Camp," by Max Oscheit.*)
RAUCH (*sings along angrily, still glaring at Speer*)
We are gypsy rovers,
Roam all round the world.
Our fair gypsy lovers
Keep our purses filled.
Down in yonder valley
We kissed and caressed.
Asked her if she'd like to —
She laughed and said "Yes."
(*The music suddenly breaks off again.*)
SPEER (*even more bitchily*) And your employee over there?
RAUCH (*bawls at him*) No need to get jealous! (*gets up and staggers over to Schürzinger*)

SCENE 80

RAUCH Mr. —
SCHÜRZINGER (*stands up*) Schürzinger.
RAUCH That's right! A striking name! (*sticks a cigar in Schürzinger's mouth*) Have another cigar. A perfect evening.
SCHÜRZINGER Just perfect, Mr. Rauch.
RAUCH Talking of perfect, do you know the story about Louis the Fifteenth, the king of France? Listen. One evening Louis the Fifteenth went with his lieutenant and the lieutenant's fiancée to the riding school. And the lieutenant left very soon after because he felt honored his monarch seemed to be somehow interested in his fiancée. — Honored! He felt honored.
(*silence*)
SCHÜRZINGER Yes, the story's not unknown to me. The lieutenant became a captain soon after —
RAUCH He did? I'd never heard that before.
(*silence*)
SCHÜRZINGER I'll say goodbye now, Mr. Rauch. (*exit*)

SCENE 81

SPEER (*comes up to Rauch; he is completely drunk*) Rauch, have you gone mad, sir, bawling at me like that? Perhaps you don't know who your'e talking to? Speer. I preside over the district court.
RAUCH Pleased to meet you.
SPEER You me too.
(*silence*)
RAUCH Werner, old pal, seems to me you're drunk.
SPEER You really mean that, Conrad?
RAUCH Definitely.
(*silence*)
SPEER The court will retire to consider its verdict. The court has no interest to declare. The sentence will not be suspended. No extenuating circumstances. The sentence will not be suspended.
RAUCH (*bitchily*) Aren't there any girls in Erfurt then?
SPEER Hardly any.
RAUCH (*with a grin*) What do people do in Erfurt, then?
SPEER (*glares at him angrily — suddenly gives him an almighty push and kicks out at him, but misses*)
(*silence*)
RAUCH Is that the end of forty years of friendship, then?
SPEER In the name of the king — (*raises his hand as if swearing an oath*) I hereby declare this separation final. Never darken my door again. (*staggers off*)

SCENE 82

RAUCH (*watching him leave*) Sad but true — another reptile. A jealous reptile. But Conrad Rauch comes from tough peasant stock. That kind of legal jargon is like water off a duck's back to him. Sixty-two years old though he may be. Ouch! (*suddenly winces and sits down on Schürzinger's chair*) What was that? — I hope I don't get any of those dizzy spells again tonight. Joseph had a hemorrhage — Just you watch out, Conrad Rauch.

SCENE 83

CAROLINE (*enters and looks round*)
(*silence*)
CAROLINE Where's Mr. Schürzinger?
RAUCH Gone. Sends you his best regards.
CAROLINE And our cavalry officer's gone too?
RAUCH We're alone.
(*silence*)
CAROLINE Are we really going to Altötting?
RAUCH Now. (*tries to stand up but has to sit down again, writhing in pain*) How much do you earn a month?
CAROLINE Fifty-five marks.
RAUCH Great.
CAROLINE I'm glad to have it.
RAUCH Given the way things are nowadays.
CAROLINE The only thing is you've got no future to look forward to. At best I might triple my salary. But by then I'll be old and gray.
RAUCH A future depends on connections (*stands up*) and Conrad Rauch Inc. is a connection. Off we go to Altötting.
(*fanfare; dark*)

SCENE 84

The orchestra plays "And When the Roses Bloom" again.

SCENE 85

The car-park in back of the Oktoberfest; a bench in the foreground. Franz Merkl enters with Erna and Casimir.

SCENE 86

FRANZ MERKL Right, this is it. There's only the one attendant and he's usually over there, because you get a better view of the fairground from there. Snap out of it, Erna!
ERNA I'm still sopping from your beer.
FRANZ MERKL I didn't really mean it seriously.
ERNA Are you sorry?
(*silence*)
FRANZ MERKL No.
(*a whistle in the distance*)
ALL THREE (*listen*)
FRANZ MERKL A cop?
ERNA Watch out, Franz.
FRANZ MERKL That's your job. Both of you keep your eyes open for anything that looks wrong. There's all kinds of expensive capitalist limousines parked here today. Tax dodgers the lot of them — (*disappears among the cars*)

SCENE 87

CASIMIR (*as if speaking to himself*) Goodbye.

SCENE 88

ERNA He's a funny guy is Franz. First of all he sends you to kingdom come then he feels sorry for it.
CASIMIR He's certainly not your Mr. Average.
ERNA That's because he's very intelligent. He can open a car door or break a window and you wouldn't hear a thing.
CASIMIR You've no choice nowadays.
ERNA You may well be right there.
(*silence*)

CASIMIR Only the day before yesterday I would have throttled anyone who had the cheek to take something out of my convertible — and now it's the other way round. The way things change!
ERNA I can't see very well tonight. I'm still dazzled by the lights.
CASIMIR That's not my problem.
(*silence*)
ERNA I often imagine a revolution — and I see all the poor people marching into Munich and the rich being taken off in Black Marias because they've been telling so many lies about the poor. In a revolution like that I wouldn't mind dying carrying the flag.
CASIMIR I would.
ERNA You know, they shot my brother in a gravelpit — in 1919 — during the revolution after the end of the war —
CASIMIR So what?
ERNA My brother sacrificed himself.
CASIMIR Then he probably enjoyed sacrificing himself.
ERNA What a stupid thing to say! Even Franz respects my brother.
(*silence*)
CASIMIR Then I must be worse than Franz Merkl.
ERNA You're just bitter.
CASIMIR I don't believe I'm a good man.
ERNA But people wouldn't be bad if the times weren't so bad. It's a downright lie that people are bad.

SCENE 89

FRANZ MERKL (*appears from between the cars carrying a briefcase and goes towards Erna menacingly*) What is it that's a downright lie now?
ERNA That people are bad.
FRANZ MERKL Oh, really.
(*silence*)
ERNA There are no people who are all bad.
FRANZ MERKL Don't make me laugh.
CASIMIR People are the product of their environment.

FRANZ MERKL There. A briefcase. (*takes a book out of it and reads out the title*) "The Erotic Complex." And an envelope. Addressed to Conrad Rauch Esquire— I think we should give Conrad Rauch Esquire his volume back. (*to Erna*) Or perhaps you're interested in this erotic complex?
ERNA No.
FRANZ MERKL Okay then.
CASIMIR Me neither.
FRANZ MERKL Very noble of you. — But you have to walk up and down, the pair of you. People'll notice if you just stand there, rooted to the spot. (*disappears again between the automobiles*)

SCENE 90

ERNA Come on then, up and down —
CASIMIR Please forgive me.
ERNA What for?
CASIMIR I've just been thinking about it. It really showed a total lack of respect, what I said about your brother who was killed.
(*silence*)
ERNA I knew you'd come round to see it that way, Casimir.
(*exit together*)

SCENE 91

The orchestra plays Schubert's "Marche militaire" (op. 51, no.1) and for a long time there is no one to be seen; then Speer enters with Elli and Maria; he has sobered up a little, but is still pretty drunk. The orchestra breaks off in the middle of a bar.

SCENE 92

MARIA No, this is the parking place for private cars, the taxis are over there by the first-aid post.

ELLI (*suddenly falls back*)
SPEER What's wrong with our blonde bombshell now!
MARIA I don't know what's wrong with her. She quite often gets these moods where she refuses to play along. (*calls out*) Elli.
ELLI (*doesn't answer*)
MARIA Come on Elli!
ELLI (*doesn't move*)
SPEER In the name of the German people!
MARIA I'll get her. (*goes over to Elli*)

SCENE 93

MARIA (*to Elli*) Don't be so stupid.
ELLI No. I'm not going to do it.
SPEER (*tries to listen but can't hear anything*)
MARIA Well, I like that. One minute you're all sauce and come-hither looks to anything in trousers, the next you're chickening out. Don't be such a big baby. We'll get ten marks. Five for you and five for me. Think of all those unpaid bills for a minute. (*silence*)
ELLI He's a pervert, the old goat.
MARIA Oh come on, it's only a bit of oral sex.
SPEER (*in a senile tone*) Elli! Elli! Elleee! — Elleee!
MARIA Come on, calm down now. (*leads Elli over to Speer; exit*)

SCENE 94

For a time there's no one to be seen and the orchestra takes up Schubert's "Marche militaire" again, then Rauch appears with Caroline. They stop beside a luxury convertible and he looks for the keys. Once again the orchestra breaks off in the middle of a bar.

SCENE 95

CAROLINE But that's an Austro-Daimler!
RAUCH Got it in one. Well done.
CAROLINE My ex-fiancé used to drive an Austro-Daimler. He was a chauffeur, you know. Three months ago we went for a spin out in the country — and he had one hell of a dustup with a carter for beating his horse. Just imagine, all because of some nag! And him a chauffeur as well! That's quite something.
RAUCH (*finally finds the key and holds the door open for her and bows*) Madam —

SCENE 96

CASIMIR (*walks past again with Erna; he sees Caroline — they recognize and stare at each other*)

SCENE 97

CAROLINE (*leaves Rauch and goes up to Casimir*) Goodbye, Casimir.
CASIMIR Goodbye.
CAROLINE Yes. And all the best.
CASIMIR Cheers.
(*silence*)
CAROLINE I'm off to Altötting.
CASIMIR Bon voyage.
(*silence*)
CASIMIR That's a swell convertible there. I used to drive one just like that. Until the day before yesterday.
RAUCH (*as above*) Madam —
CAROLINE (*slowly leaves Casimir and gets in the car with Rauch — soon the convertible has disappeared*)

SCENE 98

CASIMIR (*watches the convertible as it drives off; imitating Rauch*)
Madam —
(*dark*)

SCENE 99

Once more the orchestra plays Schubert's "Marche militaire," and plays it right to the end this time

SCENE 100

Outside the first-aid post. A first-aid attendant is seeing to Rauch who is sitting on a bench outside the first-aid hut and making heavy weather of swallowing two pills with a glass of water. Caroline is with him.
The air is still full of Oktoberfest music.

SCENE 101

CAROLINE (*observes Rauch*) Do you feel better now?
RAUCH (*doesn't answer, instead lies down on the bench*)
FIRST-AID ATTENDANT He's not any better yet, miss.
(*silence*)
CAROLINE Actually we were just going for a drive to Altötting when Mr. Rauch suddenly felt unwell — saliva started dripping out of his mouth and if I hadn't put the brake on at the last moment we might both been dead and done for.
FIRST-AID ATTENDANT So you saved his life.
CAROLINE Probably.
FIRST-AID ATTENDANT It's logical. You stopped the car.
CAROLINE Yes, I know all about cars. My ex-fiancé was a chauffeur.

SCENE 102

The orchestra softly plays the waltz 'Bist du's lachendes Glück' from Lehar's Count of Luxembourg *and out of the first-aid hut a stream of visitors to the Oktoberfest come with bandaged heads and limbs, dazed and hobbling — the midget and the MC among them. All set off home and the orchestra breaks off, in the middle of a bar.*

SCENE 103

CAROLINE (*in a low voice to the first-aid attendant*) What's happened? A disaster?
FIRST-AID ATTENDANT Why do you ask?
CAROLINE Did the roller-coaster collapse?
FIRST-AID ATTENDANT No, nothing like that. It was just a general brawl.
CAROLINE What about?
FIRST-AID ATTENDANT About nothing.
(*silence*)
CAROLINE About nothing! People are just wild animals.
FIRST-AID ATTENDANT They'll never change.
CAROLINE Still.
(*silence*)
FIRST-AID ATTENDANT The story is some old Casanova was getting into a taxi with two girls and he was pestered by some young hooligans. They say one of them took off his shoe and stuck it under the old lecher's nose and told him to smell it — but he refused and one of the other hooligans socked him in the face. The result was that in nought point nought seconds a hundred men were mixing it and not one of them had any idea what it was about, they all just lashed out with their fists. People are so on edge nowadays they fly off the handle at the least excuse.

SCENE 104

DOCTOR (*appears in the door of the first-aid hut*) The stretchers not here yet?
FIRST-AID ATTENDANT Not yet, sir.
DOCTOR Well, we've got six cases of concussion, one broken jaw, four broken arms, one of them a compound fracture, all the rest are flesh wounds. What a shambles! Germans fighting Germans! (*disappears*)

SCENE 105

CAROLINE A broken jaw — ouch, that must hurt.
FIRST-AID ATTENDANT Nowadays it's not that bad, given the progress of medical science.
CAROLINE But you're marked for life, as if you'd had an ear cut off. Especially for a woman.
FIRST-AID ATTENDANT It wasn't a woman who had her jaw smashed, it was the dirty old man.
CAROLINE Then it's okay.
FIRST-AID ATTENDANT He's something high up in the law, even. From North Germany. Name of Speer.
RAUCH (*has been listening and roars*) What?! (*stands up*) The law? Speer? A dirty old man?! (*clutches at his heart*)
Silence
CAROLINE Now don't start getting worked up, Mr. Rauch —
RAUCH (*shouts at her*) And what are you doing still hanging round? Goodnight and goodbye! Farewell!
(*silence*)
RAUCH A broken jaw. Poor guy, an old comrade. — These goddam women. Never touch them with a bargepole. Filthy scum! Get rid them. The lot of 'em!
CAROLINE Don't shout at me like that, I've done nothing to deserve it, Mr. Rauch —
RAUCH Deserve? That's all I needed!
(*silence*)

CAROLINE I saved your life.
RAUCH Saved my life?
(*silence*)
RAUCH (*with a grin*) You'd like that, wouldn't you —
(*silence*)
RAUCH (*to the First-Aid Attendant*) Where is Speer? Still inside?
FIRST-AID ATTENDANT Yes sir, just follow me, sir.

SCENE 106

RAUCH (*slowly makes his way over to the first-aid hut — Elli and Maria appear in the doorway, Maria with her arm in a sling, Elli with a huge bandage over her eye. Maria recognizes Rauch and stares at him; Rauch recognizes her too and stops briefly.*)

SCENE 107

MARIA (*with a grin*) Ah, little Mister Pisspot. — Look, Elli, look —

ELLI (*lifts up her head and tries to look*) Ouch, my eye!
(*silence*)
RAUCH (*adjusts his tie and walks past Elli and Maria into the first-aid hut*)
CAROLINE (*suddenly screeches*) Goodbye Mister Pisspot!
(*dark*)

SCENE 108

The orchestra plays "Bist du's lachendes Glück" again.

SCENE 109

Back in the parking lot, but a different part, where the flags of the exhibition can be seen. Casimir and Erna are still walking up and down — Casimir suddenly stops. Erna too.

SCENE 110

CASIMIR Where's Merkl got to?
ERNA Oh, he'll be somewhere.
(*silence*)
CASIMIR And where little Miss Caroline's got to I couldn't care less.
ERNA No, she wasn't the woman for you. I've got an eye for that kind of thing.
CASIMIR A woman like that's like an automobile where nothing works properly — it keeps on having to be repaired. The gas is the blood and the magneto's the heart — and if the spark's too weak the motor misfires — and if there's too much oil in the mixture, it smokes and stinks —
ERNA You certainly do have imagination! Not many men have. Franz Merkl, for example, has none at all. And you're quite right when you say he treats me unfairly — No! I'm not going to put up with it anymore — (*suddenly exclaims in a low voice*) Jesus, Joseph and Mary! Franz! Jesus and Mary — (*puts her hand over her mouth and whimpers*)
CASIMIR What's wrong?
ERNA There — they've got him, they've got Franz. Look, those two cops — Forgive me, Franz — I wasn't bitching, no, I wasn't bitching —
(*silence*)
CASIMIR It's all that slut's fault. That whore. That little Miss Caroline!
ERNA He's not resisting — just lets them take him — (*sits down on the bench*) I'll never see him again.
CASIMIR Oh come on now, they're not going to execute him.

ERNA It'll come down to the same thing, more or less. He's got a record, they'll give him five years hard labor for nothing, and that means he'll never come out — he caught tuberculosis when he was in jail before — he'll never come out.
(*silence*)
CASIMIR Have you got a previous conviction too?
ERNA Yes.
CASIMIR (*sits down beside Erna*)
(*silence*)
ERNA How old do you think I am?
CASIMIR Twenty-five.
ERNA Twenty.
CASIMIR Nowadays we're all older than we are.
(*silence*)
CASIMIR There's Franz now.
ERNA (*starts*) Where?
(*silence*)

SCENE 111

Franz Merkl goes past with a detective, handcuffed to his wrist — he gives Erna one last look.

SCENE 112

(*silence*)
ERNA Poor Franz. Poor soul.
CASIMIR That's life.
ERNA You've hardly begun and it's over.
CASIMIR I've always said there's no point to criminal acts like that — I think I'll look on Franz Merkl as a timely warning.
ERNA Better to go on the dole.
CASIMIR Better to go hungry.
ERNA Yes.
(*silence*)

ERNA I told poor Franz to leave you in peace. I could sense straight away that you were different — that's why he sloshed the beer in my face.
CASIMIR That was why?
ERNA Yes. Because of you.
CASIMIR I didn't know that. That you — that because of me — Am I really worth it?
ERNA That I can't say.
(*silence*)
CASIMIR Is that the Big Dipper up there?
ERNA Yes. And that's Orion.
CASIMIR With his sword.
ERNA (*with a quiet smile*) You remembered —
(*silence*)
CASIMIR (*still staring up at the sky*) It just happens to be an imperfect world.
ERNA One could certainly imagine it a bit more perfect.
CASIMIR How's your health? I mean, did you catch tuberculosis from poor old Franz?
ERNA No. So far I'm perfectly healthy.
(*silence*)
CASIMIR I think we're kindred spirits.
ERNA I feel as if we've known each other for ages.
CASIMIR What was your brother called? The one that died?
ERNA Ludwig. Ludwig Reitmeier.
(*silence*)
CASIMIR I used to be a chauffeur for someone called Reitmeier. He ran a woolen goods business. Wholesale. (*puts his arm round her shoulders*)
ERNA (*leans her head against his chest*) There's Caroline.

SCENE 113

CAROLINE (*enters and looks round, as if she's looking for someone — sees Casimir and Erna, slowly goes over to them and stops right in front of the bench*) Hello, Casimir.

(*silence*)
CAROLINE Don't keep giving me those ironic looks.
CASIMIR Any woman can say that.
Silence
CAROLINE You were right.
CASIMIR How do you mean?
CAROLINE Actually I just wanted to have an ice — then the Zeppelin flew past and I had a go on the roller-coaster. Then you said I'll leave you because you're out of work. It's automatic, you said.
CASIMIR That's right, ma'am.
(*silence*)
CAROLINE I imagined I could get myself some rosier future prospects — for a while I had all kinds of ideas. But I had to stoop so low to rise in the world. For example, I saved Mr. Rauch's life and he just doesn't want to know.
CASIMIR That's right, ma'am.
(*silence*)
CAROLINE You said Rauch was just using me for his own pleasure and I belonged with you — and you were quite right there.
CASIMIR I couldn't care less! That's all behind me now. Dead is dead and there's no such thing as ghosts, especially not between the sexes.
(*silence*)
CAROLINE (*suddenly gives him a kiss*)
CASIMIR Get back! Ugh! Yuck! (*spits out*) Yuck!
ERNA I don't understand how a woman can show so little sensitivity.
CAROLINE (*to Casimir*) Is this the new Caroline?
CASIMIR What the fuck is it to do with you?
CAROLINE And going behind Franz Merkl's back, does that show sensitivity?
ERNA Franz Merkl's dead.
(*silence*)
CAROLINE Dead? (*laughs, but suddenly breaks off; to Erna, bitchily*) And you expect me to believe that, jailbird?
CASIMIR Shut your face and push off.

ERNA (*to Casimir*) Just ignore her. She doesn't know what she's doing.
(*silence*)

SCENE 114

CAROLINE (*aside*) You get such a yearning inside you sometimes — but then you go back with broken wings and life's going on as if you'd never been there —

SCENE 115

SCHÜRZINGER (*enters, in high spirits — with a balloon on a string in his buttonhole; sees Caroline*) Well, well, if this isn't a sight for Eugene's poor old eyes? It's destiny that we run into each other again, Caroline. The day after tomorrow Lieutenant Schürzinger will be First Lieutenant Schürzinger — in the army of His Majesty Louis the Fifteenth — and it's you I've to thank for it.
CAROLINE There must be some mistake.
SCHÜRZINGER Nonsense.
(*silence*)
CAROLINE Eugene, I hurt your feelings and you shouldn't do that because you get paid back for everything —
SCHÜRZINGER You need someone, Caroline —
CAROLINE It's always the same shit.
SCHÜRZINGER No! Everything's getting better and better.
CAROLINE Who says so?
SCHÜRZINGER Coué.
(*silence*)
SCHÜRZINGER Okay now, repeat after me: Everything's getting better —
CAROLINE (*repeats in a toneless voice*) Everything's getting better —
SCHÜRZINGER Everything's getting better and better, better and better —

CAROLINE Everything's getting better and better — and better —
SCHÜRZINGER (*embraces her and gives her a long kiss*)
CAROLINE (*doesn't resist*)
SCHÜRZINGER You really do need someone.
CAROLINE (*smiles*) Everything's getting better and better
SCHÜRZINGER Come on — *exit together*

SCENE 116

CASIMIR Dreams — who needs 'em.
ERNA As long as we don't string ourselves up we won't starve.
(*silence*)
CASIMIR Hey, Erna —
ERNA What?
CASIMIR Nothing.
(*silence*)

SCENE 117

ERNA (*sings softly - eventually Casimir joins in too*)
But when the roses blossom
All our sorrow departs
For the season of roses
Brings love to our hearts.
Ev'ry year when the spring comes
We know winter is gone,
But the roses of Maytime
Flow'r for us once alone.

Faith, Love, Hope

A Little Dance of Death in Five Acts

Written with the Collaboration of Lukas Kristl

Faith, Love, Hope

Note:

Passing through Munich in February 1932, I met an acquaintance of mine called Lukas Kristl who for some years had been reporting on court proceedings for a local newspaper. What he said to me was roughly the following: I don't understand you dramatists. I don't understand why, when you make a play out of a crime and its consequences, you almost always prefer so-called capital offenses, which are relatively rare. Why do you dramatists almost never look at the petty crimes we come across all over the country all the time in a thousand different shapes and forms? Very often the cause is mere ignorance but just as often the consequences can be similar to those of lifelong imprisonment or even the death penalty.

Then Kristl told me of a case he had come across in the course of his work as a reporter, and the case was turned into the little dance of death, *Faith, Love, Hope*. Kristl was personally acquainted with the real people behind Elizabeth, the policeman (Alfred Klostermeyer), the judge's wife, and the inspector, and I would like to express my thanks to him for making this material available to me, and for all the suggestions he made.

Kristl's idea was to write a play attacking the mindless bureaucratic insistence on petty regulations, regardless of the consequences — recognizing, of course, that there will always be petty regulations simply because any society, whatever its form, needs them. What Kristl hoped to achieve was that people might perhaps apply these petty regulations more humanely.

That was my intention too. However, it was of course clear to me that this "attack on petty regulations" was merely the subject matter, allowing me once more to show the gigantic struggle between individual and society, that eternal conflict that can never be resolved; at best an individual might for a few moments enjoy the illusion of a truce.

As in all my plays, I have in this little dance of death constantly borne in mind that the individual's hopeless struggle is grounded in their animal instincts, and that consequently the heroic and cowardly manner of the struggle must be seen as deriving from our animal nature which, as is well known, is neither good nor evil.

As in all my plays, here too I have not tried to make things appear better or worse than they are. Anyone who attempts to portray men and women with an open mind and an open eye will doubtless recognize (unless his knowledge of human beings is second-hand) that our expressions of feeling have been sentimentalized, that is trivialized and adulterated and filled with a masochistic lust for pity, probably as a result of our combination of attention-seeking and indolence. Anyone, then, who makes an honest attempt to portray men and women will find that what he creates is mere reflections, but I would like to emphasize that I have never created reflections of men and women just for a laugh, nor will I ever do so; parody is something I reject.

As in all my plays, here too I have tried to be as ruthless in my treatment of stupidity and dishonesty as possible. Such ruthlessness must be the foremost task of a writer who sometimes imagines the sole aim of his writing is to get people to know themselves. Know thyself, I beg you, that you may acquire that serenity which will ease your struggle with life and death; your honesty will place you, not above yourself (that would be an illusion), but beside and below yourself, so that even if you cannot view yourself from on high, at least you can do so from in front, from behind, from the side, and from below!

Faith, Love, Hope could be the title of each one of my plays. And I could have prefaced each one of them with the following quotation from the Bible:

And when the LORD smelled the pleasing odor, the LORD said in his heart: "I will never again curse the ground because of man, for the imagination of man's heart is evil from his youth; neither will I ever again destroy every living creature as I have done. While the earth remains, seedtime and harvest, cold and heat, summer and winter, day and night, shall not cease."

Genesis 8, 21

CHARACTERS

ELIZABETH
POLICE OFFICER (ALFRED KLOSTERMEYER)
SENIOR TECHNICIAN AT THE ANATOMICAL INSTITUTE
TECHNICIAN AT THE ANATOMICAL INSTITUTE
LABORATORY ASSISTANT AT THE ANATOMICAL INSTITUTE
BARON WITH A BLACK ARMBAND
MRS. PRANTL
THE JUDGE'S WIFE
HIS HONOR, THE JUDGE
DISABLED WORKER
LABORER'S WIFE
BOOKKEEPER
MARIA
PLAINCLOTHES POLICEMAN
POLICE CAPTAIN
A SECOND POLICE OFFICER (KLOSTERMEYER'S BUDDY)
A THIRD POLICE OFFICER
JOE, THE INTREPID YOUNG LIFESAVER

ACT ONE

SCENE 1

Outside the frosted-glass windows of the Anatomical Institute in Munich.
Elizabeth is about to enter. She has one final look round, but not a soul is to be seen.
In the distance an orchestra starts to play Chopin's popular "Funeral March," and a young police officer (Alfred Klostermeyer) slowly walks past Elizabeth, apparently paying hardly any attention to her.
It is spring.

SCENE 2

ELIZABETH (*suddenly addresses the Police Officer; the funeral march in the distance slowly fades*) Pardon me, but I'm looking for the Anatomical Institute.
POLICE OFFICER The Anatomical Institute?
ELIZABETH Where they chop up the corpses.
POLICE OFFICER That's it there.
ELIZABETH Oh, thank you, that's all I wanted to know.
(*silence*)
POLICE OFFICER (*with a smile*) Just you watch out — they've rows and rows of heads in there.
ELIZABETH I'm not afraid of the dead.
POLICE OFFICER Me neither.
ELIZABETH It takes a lot to scare me.
POLICE OFFICER In that case — (*gives a casual salute and goes off*)

SCENE 3

Elizabeth watches him leave, with a mocking expression on her face, then she screws up her courage and rings the bell of the Anatomical Institute. It can be heard ringing inside, then the

Technician appears in his white lab coat. He stands in the doorway staring at Elizabeth, who seems unable to make up her mind.

SCENE 4

TECHNICIAN Yes?
ELIZABETH I'd like to speak to somebody in charge.
TECHNICIAN What's it about?
ELIZABETH It's urgent.
TECHNICIAN Have we the body of someone you're related to?
ELIZABETH I've not come about a dead body, I've come about myself.
TECHNICIAN How do you mean?
ELIZABETH Are you in charge here?
TECHNICIAN I'm the technician. You can tell me what it's all about.
(*silence*)
ELIZABETH I've been told — someone specifically told me — that you can sell your body here — that is, after I'm dead you gentlemen can do what you like with my body — for scientific purposes, of course — but I get the fee immediately. Now, that is.
TECHNICIAN That's news to me.
ELIZABETH But someone specifically told me.
TECHNICIAN Who?
ELIZABETH Someone at work.
TECHNICIAN What d'you do for a living, then?
ELIZABETH At the moment nothing, really. People say things are going to get worse, but I'm not going to let that get me down.
(*silence*)
TECHNICIAN Selling your own corpse — what will people think of next?
ELIZABETH It can't just go on like this for ever.
TECHNICIAN How wrong can you be? (*takes a bag of bird food out of his pocket and feeds the pigeons that fly down from the roof of the Anatomical Institute. The pigeons know the Technician; they perch on his shoulders and eat out of his hand*)

SCENE 5

The Senior Technician appears; he is seeing the Baron with a black armband to the door of the anatomical Institute.
SENIOR TECHNICIAN   Certainly Baron, it'll be done straight away. And once again, my heartfelt condolences.
BARON   Thank you, thank you. I still reproach myself for what happened, you know.
SENIOR TECHNICIAN   But the district attorney's investigation proved any accusations against you were groundless, Baron. The Lord giveth and the Lord taketh away.
BARON   I was at Verdun and on the Somme, but yesterday's catastrophe was worse than anything I've had to go through. Only married three months, and I was at the wheel when the accident happened — going round that bend. On that twisty road between Lechbruck and Steingaden. I'm just glad they've released the body.
SENIOR TECHNICIAN   (*noticing the Technician*) One moment, please. (*goes over to the Technician and shouts at him*) Feeding the pigeons again?! What do you think you're doing? It's like a pigsty in there! Fingers and gullets lying about all over the place! Get those two hearts and the half spleen put away in the drawer at once! It really is a disgrace in there, goddammit!
TECHNICIAN   But this young lady was asking if she could sell her corpse, sir —
SENIOR TECHNICIAN   Her corpse? Not another one?
(*silence*)
BARON   Unbelievable!
SENIOR TECHNICIAN   God knows how many times we've issued denials but people just won't believe official announcements. They imagine the state is willing to lay out good money for their corpse while it's still alive! As if their bodies were of any interest to anyone! And it's always the state has to pay out, the state!
BARON   Unbelievable what people believe the state is there for!
SENIOR TECHNICIAN   There's going to be changes, Baron.
BARON   Let's hope so.

SCENE 6

LABORATORY ASSISTANT (*appearing at the door of the Institute carrying the Senior Technician's hat*) Sir! Telephone message, sir!
SENIOR TECHNICIAN Who for? Me?
LABORATORY ASSISTANT It's the report on that Leopoldine Hackinger from Brno. The professor wants you to go over to the clinic right away. (*hands him his hat*)
SENIOR TECHNICIAN Right away! (*hurriedly takes off his white coat and hands it to the Assistant, who goes back into the Institute; to the Baron*) You will excuse me, Baron, won't you? Our experts obviously can't work out what it was the woman died from. A Sudeten German, you know. Duty calls —
BARON Of course.
SENIOR TECHNICIAN And once again, my sincere condolences.
BARON Thank you.
SENIOR TECHNICIAN It was a pleasure, Baron. (*dashes off, to the right*)
BARON Goodbye. (*goes off slowly, to the left; a few bars of Chopin's Funeral March are heard in the distance again.*
It is already late afternoon, and it slowly starts to get dark)

SCENE 7

TECHNICIAN (*watching the Senior Technician leave*) Heartless. The poor pigeons. Believe me, miss, the best thing would be to throw yourself out of the window.
ELIZABETH Oh, you're too kind.
TECHNICIAN No, really, I have your best interests at heart. Who's going to buy a corpse? Nowadays?!
ELIZABETH There's always tomorrow.
TECHNICIAN Things won't change.
ELIZABETH I don't believe that.
TECHNICIAN So you believe —?
ELIZABETH (*with a smile*) I believe fortune's going to smile on me some day, and I'm not going to let you take that away from me. If

I'd managed to sell my corpse, for example, for a hundred and fifty marks, for example.
TECHNICIAN (*interrupts her*) A hundred and fifty marks?
ELIZABETH Yes.
(*silence*)
TECHNICIAN (*with a grin*) You child —
ELIZABETH Pardon. What do you mean?
TECHNICIAN What does your father do for a living?
ELIZABETH He's an inspector.
TECHNICIAN An inspector? That's quite something.
ELIZABETH But he can't help me out because Mama passed away in March and he had a lot of expenses to do with that.
TECHNICIAN What's a lousy senior technician compared with an inspector, miss? Now that really is something.
ELIZABETH You see, if I had a hundred and fifty marks I could get my license to work as a door-to-door saleswoman and the world would be my oyster. If I had my license I could walk into a position tomorrow where I'd be as good as my own boss — in the same branch I used to work in before the bad times came and put a stop to it.
TECHNICIAN What branch would that be?
ELIZABETH Girdles, corsets. Wholesale. Brassieres and that kind of thing as well.
TECHNICIAN Interesting.
(*silence*)
ELIZABETH Where are the days of wine and roses?
(*silence*)
TECHNICIAN (*takes a photo out of his wallet*) there, take a look st that —
ELIZABETH (*looks at the photo*) A nice dog.
TECHNICIAN My terrier.
ELIZABETH Looks bright and lively.
TECHNICIAN And fierce! Unfortunately he died.
ELIZABETH Pity.
TECHNICIAN (*whistles*) That was his whistle. He always came to that. (*talking to the photo*) My little Laddie — now you've gone —

no more walkies. (*puts the photo back in his wallet; to Elizabeth*) You felt sorry for poor little Laddie, I like that. What's your name?
ELIZABETH Elizabeth.
Silence.
TECHNICIAN The Empress Elizabeth of Austria — she was a fine filly, and still she was murdered by a scoundrel of an assassin. In Geneva. Where that League of Nations — scoundrels the lot of 'em. — All I have left now is my butterfly collection and my canary, and yesterday I was adopted by a cat. Would you be interested in seeing an aquarium?
ELIZABETH Pardon?
TECHNICIAN I have a terrarium too.
ELIZABETH That's more my kind of thing.
TECHNICIAN Why don't you come round and see me then, little Miss Inspector?
ELIZABETH Perhaps.

SCENE 8

The Senior Technician returns from the clinic — sooner than expected (there is a large bandage round his finger); he sees the Technician, stops short, outraged, and fixes him with a baleful stare; the Technician shrinks back, and Elizabeth retires a short distance.

SCENE 9

SENIOR TECHNICIAN (*slowly goes up to the Technician and stops right in front of him*) Again? Feeding the pigeons again, are we? (*suddenly bellows at him*) I don't want to see you out here anymore! (*to Elizabeth*) D'you hear me?!
ELIZABETH I certainly do. (*exit*)

SCENE 10

SENIOR TECHNICIAN (*watching Elizabeth go*) A fine state of affairs we have here! Instead of getting round to cataloging those tumors

at last, here you are whiling away the time with some young wench!
TECHNICIAN You're wrong there, sir. She's a young lady; she's the daughter of a customs inspector who's fallen on hard times.
SENIOR TECHNICIAN A customs inspector, eh?
TECHNICIAN Yes, sir. And if that customs inspector had a hundred and fifty marks, then she'd have her saleswoman's license and the world would be her oyster. I know you think I'm incompetent, sir, because I keep an aquarium — and feed the pigeons — and have a kind heart —
SENIOR TECHNICIAN Get to the point!
TECHNICIAN The point is, sir, that I'm going to help this customs inspector's daughter out. I've made up my mind. A hundred and fifty marks.
SENIOR TECHNICIAN A hundred and fifty?
TECHNICIAN The young lady will pay it back.
SENIOR TECHNICIAN Seems to me you still believe in miracles, you're just another pigeon yourself. If you were my wife I'd soon teach you to throw your money away. (*threatens him teasingly with his bandaged finger*)
TECHNICIAN What's wrong with your finger? Cut?
SENIOR TECHNICIAN Infected.
TECHNICIAN Not from a corpse, I hope.
SENIOR TECHNICIAN Of course it's from a corpse. Just now. That complicated case from the Sudetenland.
TECHNICIAN I'd keep a good eye on it if I were you, sir.
(*silence*)
SENIOR TECHNICIAN (*examining his bandaged finger*) It doesn't hurt, that's what's worrying me —
TECHNICIAN Now when I look at my butterfly collection, for example, I always tell myself there's a higher being that orders things.
SENIOR TECHNICIAN Come on, it's time we got back to work. Duty calls! (*goes into the Institute with the Technician. Dark*)

ACT TWO

SCENE 1

The office of Mrs. Prantl's corsetry firm. Mrs. Prantl is a gossipy type, especially in her business dealings. At the moment she is sitting at her desk shuffling papers about, making herself look important. In the background are waxwork figures with corsets, girdles, brassieres and the like, lined up in a row, like the heads in the Anatomical Institute.

MRS. PRANTL Remarkable, really remarkable! Seven girdles, six corsets, eleven garter belts in just three days! Well done. You've got a talent for it, I must say! More than many professional saleswomen. A genius!
JUDGE'S WIFE Too kind, my dear, too kind — one moves in certain social circles and people are happy to oblige a judge's wife —
MRS. PRANTL Too modest, my dear, too modest! Selling's an uphill business these days. People just slam the door in your face.
JUDGE'S WIFE But we do have our agreement, don't we? If anyone should ask, then of course you'll say I'm selling these things just to pass the time, as it were —
MRS. PRANTL Goes without saying! I mean it's our little secret, and that's the way it'll stay.
JUDGE'S WIFE In difficult times like these one has to help one's husband out. He still earns his six hundred marks a month, but there's one cut-back after another, and those fine gentlemen at their comfortable desks in the ministry — (*the telephone rings and she breaks off*)
MRS. PRANTL (*at the telephone*) Yes, send her straight in. (*to the Judge's Wife*) This'll only take a moment, then we can get back to our chat.

SCENE 2

ELIZABETH (*enters*)
MRS. PRANTL Morning. Come in and let's see it — have you managed your quota?
ELIZABETH There you are. (*hands her order book to Mrs. Prantl*)
MRS. PRANTL (*leafing through it*) What?! Two garter belts, one girdle and one corset! That's less than nothing!
ELIZABETH Selling's an uphill business these days. People just slam the door in your face.
MRS. PRANTL None of your tired clichés, please. As a saleswoman it's your job to inculcate a sense of beauty in our customers. Nowadays, when everyone's exercising, when you can see naked women everywhere, that's the best kind of advertising for our products. You should concentrate on the gentlemen more, I've yet to meet a man who could resist a garter belt. How did you get on in Kaufbeuren?
ELIZABETH There was nothing doing in Kaufbeuren.
MRS. PRANTL What do you mean, nothing doing? Sales have always been phenomenal in Kaufbeuren.
ELIZABETH I didn't get to Kaufbeuren.
MRS. PRANTL So where did you get to, then?
ELIZABETH I wanted to save time, so I took a car — and a rather direct route, then the oil ran out and I had to spend the night in a barn in the woods.
MRS. PRANTL (*scolding*) In the woods?! Do you think I pay you for nothing? You can keep on taking those direct routes till kingdom come and you still won't have paid off the hundred and fifty marks I advanced you for your license!
ELIZABETH But it was an act of God.
MRS. PRANTL If my employees are going to start coming up with acts of God, then it's time I retired! Blood poisoning or falling off a streetcar and breaking your leg, I can accept that, but an act of God is a luxury I've never allowed myself, never mind my employees!
ELIZABETH But I couldn't help it.

MRS. PRANTL Don't give me that puppy-dog look, little Miss Act-of-God! Look at this lady here instead. She's a judge's wife and she doesn't have to do it, it's just a pastime for her and she's sold four times as much as you.

SCENE 3

TECHNICIAN (*rushes in and immediately starts shouting at Elizabeth; he is beside himself with rage*) So there you are, you swindler! You fraud! Your father's not a customs inspector at all. If you'd said straight away he wasn't a customs inspector but just inspected damaged goods for some lousy insurance firm do you think I'd have given you the money to set you up?
ELIZABETH But I never claimed —
TECHNICIAN (*interrupting her*) Oh yes you did!
ELIZABETH No, I didn't!
TECHNICIAN (*slamming his walking-stick down on Mrs. Prantl's desk, so that her papers flutter all over the place, and bellowing*) Customs inspector! Customs inspector! Customs inspector!
MRS. PRANTL (*gathering up her papers; shrieks*) Stop it! Stop it! (*silence*)
TECHNICIAN (*with a gallant bow to Mrs. Prantl and the Judge's Wife*) Do excuse me, ladies, for descending on you like this, but compared with an insurance clerk who inspects damaged goods, even a lousy senior technician's a somebody, and that little minx there induced me to part with my hard-earned cash —
ELIZABETH (*interrupts him*) That's not true!
MRS. PRANTL Silence!
TECHNICIAN Silence!
MRS. PRANTL (*wagging her finger at Elizabeth*) Young lady, young lady — shouting only shows you're in the wrong.
TECHNICIAN (*shouting*) In the wrong! Yes!
(*silence*)
ELIZABETH I'm not saying another word.
TECHNICIAN (*scathingly*) How very convenient for you.
MRS. PRANTL (*to the Technician*) Won't you sit down?

TECHNICIAN Thank you. (*sits down*) I'm a really kind-hearted person, you know, but if there's one thing I can't stand, it's people telling lies.
ELIZABETH I didn't tell a lie.
MRS. PRANTL Do you think you could hold your tongue, missy, just for one minute —
TECHNICIAN I should think so, too.
MRS. PRANTL (*offers the Technician a cigarette*) Would you —
TECHNICIAN I don't mind if I do. (*lights up, leans back in his chair blowing out the smoke appreciatively*) Well, ladies, this is the way it was. This — this person comes and visits me in my home, and wangles her way into my fatherly affection, and I show her my aquarium and lend her a book on Tibet — and buy her license for her into the bargain. And all the time her father's not a customs inspector at all! I made inquiries, you see, just for my own personal peace of mind. People around me are always making fun of me because I'm so soft-hearted.
MRS. PRANTL License? Not a license to work as a door-to-door saleswoman? But I paid for that?!
TECHNICIAN What?! You paid for one too?
MRS. PRANTL That's standard practice. The firm finances the employee's license, so they can work, and the employee gradually pays it off. A hundred and fifty marks.
TECHNICIAN (*beside himself*) A hundred and fifty marks?!
(*silence*)
MRS. PRANTL That's fraud.
ELIZABETH (*suddenly bursts out*) I'm not a swindler!
JUDGE'S WIFE That's not the point, young lady. The point is, do your actions constitute fraud, that's the point. Otherwise where would we be? The courts might as well shut up shop.
MRS. PRANTL Quite right.
JUDGE'S WIFE It's none of my business and I've never had anything to do with the courts myself, thank God — apart from being married to a judge, that is, and when I hear you didn't use the money this gentleman gave you to pay for your license, then I can hear my Augustus saying, "False pretenses — constitutes fraud."

TECHNICIAN (*bowed down in despair; whining*) I'm just a poor laboratory technician who's done a good deed —
ELIZABETH But sir, don't worry, you'll get your money back.
TECHNICIAN No.
ELIZABETH You will, every penny.
TECHNICIAN When?
ELIZABETH I'll pay it off from my earnings.
MRS. PRANTL From your earnings?! (*reads from Elizabeth's order book*) Two garter belts, one girdle and one corset. And one act of God!
TECHNICIAN (*suddenly starting up*) "Act of God!"? Act of deceit! You give me my money back, on the spot!
ELIZABETH I haven't got it at the moment.
MRS. PRANTL But you paid for your license with my money!
ELIZABETH Yes, that's true.
TECHNICIAN There! You see!
ELIZABETH There was something more urgent I needed this gentleman's money for.
MRS. PRANTL Curiouser and curiouser!
ELIZABETH Well if you must know, I needed it to pay a fine.
TECHNICIAN (*beside himself again*) What?! You've already been in trouble with the law?! You've got a record?! Well, you're going to end up in prison this time, you take my word for it. I'll be the last victim of your wiles! (*dashes off*)

SCENE 4

MRS. PRANTL A fine kettle of fish!
JUDGE'S WIFE If that gentleman swears under oath you said your father was a customs inspector when he's just some kind of insurance clerk, then you're in for it.
MRS. PRANTL Hard labor!
JUDGE'S WIFE That's going a bit far. But you'll be sent to prison. Fourteen days without the option, I'd say.
ELIZABETH And everyone will think I've done something really bad.

MRS. PRANTL People are free to think what they like — especially if you hide the fact that you've got a criminal record from them.
ELIZABETH But I'm not obliged to reveal that to you.
MRS. PRANTL Don't come all hoity-toity with me, my girl! It's a scandal, a disgrace! You're dismissed of course, on the spot — and you stay there until the police come. (*exit*)

SCENE 5

JUDGE'S WIFE It's none of my business, but it's always pretty bad once you've got criminal record.
ELIZABETH (*like a schoolgirl repeating a lesson*) I was convicted for working as a traveling saleswoman without a license. They fined me one hundred and fifty marks, payable in installments. I got behind with them and the whole lot was due or I'd have to go to jail — and that would have really done for my future prospects. That's what I used that gentleman's money for.
JUDGE'S WIFE Take my advice and don't waste your time denying things, and don't try to appear cleverer than the judge. My husband's a decent fellow, but don't drag the proceedings out by wasting your time defending yourself. If I'm sitting waiting at home and his lunch is getting cold and he can't get away because the case is taking such a long time, well, even he starts to run out of patience. Those in the dock should remember the judge's only human too.
(*dark*)

ACT THREE

SCENE 1

The minuscule garden outside the welfare agency.
A discussion is going on among a group of applicants, a laborer's wife, a middle-aged bookkeeper and a girl called Maria. Elizabeth is there too. She is leaning back against the bars round the little garden, sunning herself in the weak, late-afternoon sunshine.
A disabled worker hobbles out of the welfare agency.

SCENE 2

DISABLED WORKER Isn't that just great!? Now the Welfare tell me it's not their responsibility. I have to go somewhere else — again, for Christ's sake!
LABORER'S WIFE You should go to the disability insurance office.
DISABLED WORKER The insurance people say it's none of their business, it's my labor association should be dealing with it. The labor association says my legs were bad before the accident, because I already had varicose veins and flat feet — and their specialist told me to my face I could have been walking without a stick for ages if I wanted to.
BOOKKEEPER Have you tried the arbitration panel?
DISABLED WORKER They just confirmed the labor association's decision to reduce my payments from sixty to forty percent. They actually wrote in their report that the applicant lacked motivation to return to work because he didn't earn much more when he had a job than he does now with his pension.

SCENE 3

They suddenly all go quiet and don't move while a policeman (Alfred Klostermeyer) walks slowly past, apparently not paying them the least attention. It is already slowly starting to get dark.

SCENE 4

LABORER'S WIFE (*watching the policeman disappear*) General Nose-in-the-air —
BOOKKEEPER Give us this day our daily bread.
MARIA I'm even worse off.
DISABLED WORKER Worse off?
MARIA There's seven of us in the family, you see — with an eighth on the way — but because my father brings home forty marks a week, they deduct something from my welfare.
DISABLED WORKER Cheats, the lot of them!
ELIZABETH They won't give me anything because my father's still earning.
BOOKKEEPER What is your father?
ELIZABETH Inspector with an insurance company. (*laughs*)
LABORER'S WIFE What're you laughing at? You weak in the head or something?
ELIZABETH (*stops laughing abruptly*)
LABORER'S WIFE Why don't you go home to him, then?
ELIZABETH No!
LABORER'S WIFE Then you've only got yourself to blame. Her father's an inspector —
ELIZABETH (*interrupts her*) With an insurance company! He's just a kind of clerk.
LABORER'S WIFE An inspector's an inspector.
ELIZABETH (*grinning*) And who are you to say?
BOOKKEEPER Pride and stupidity grow on the same tree.
LABORER'S WIFE Has a home to go to and doesn't take advantage of it!
ELIZABETH There's a particular reason for it.
LABORER'S WIFE You been in trouble with the law?
ELIZABETH Do I look like I have?
(*silence*)
BOOKKEEPER (*with a grin*) All that glitters is not gold. (*exit*)

SCENE 5

MARIA (*to Elizabeth*) The things we have to put up with!.
ELIZABETH Don't remind me.

SCENE 6

DISABLED WORKER (*counting off on his fingers*) Welfare agency. Workfare. Labor association. Disability insurance. Arbitration panel. — See you in the mass grave! (*exit*)

SCENE 7

LABORER'S WIFE (*aside*) Mass grave — how long before there's a place in one for you? (*exit*)

SCENE 8

MARIA What was it you did?
ELIZABETH Nothing.
MARIA But they still chucked you in jail?
ELIZABETH (*says nothing*)
MARIA You can tell me, I know how these things happen. There's a tangle of petty regulations and you get stuck in them. It's all over before you know what's happening. They gave my father ten days for a first offense because he stole a few planks from the building site. They were just lying around and we live in a wooden shack and the rain was pouring in on our beds. If you're going to risk getting caught then it might as well be for something worthwhile.
ELIZABETH (*remains silent; night has fallen and the two women are sitting by themselves on the base of the railings round the tiny garden, by the light from the welfare agency windows*)
MARIA Been married?
ELIZABETH No.
(*silence*)
ELIZABETH You know, my father and me, we're like chalk and cheese. For example, when I was born he was furious that I was

just a girl. He's always held it against me. Yet he gives himself airs, pretends to be so sophisticated. If my mother weren't dead she'd have a sorry tale to tell. All men are totally self-centered.
MARIA You just haven't met Mr. Right, that's what it is.
ELIZABETH Could be.
MARIA He'll come along one day. When you're least expecting it.
(*silence*)
ELIZABETH Give me ten thousand men and at most there'll be one I like.
MARIA I can believe that.
ELIZABETH I always wanted to be independent — my own master, so to speak.
MARIA Impossible.
(*silence*)
MARIA I wouldn't object if some man would marry me. As long as he didn't beat me, that's all. — What are you doing at the moment?
ELIZABETH Nothing.
(*silence*)
MARIA (*suddenly stands up*) Hey, come on! Let's have a look over there. The man in that café, I bet he'll stand us a ham sandwich.
ELIZABETH No, not that.
(*silence*)
MARIA Why not?
ELIZABETH Because. Too much self-respect.
(*silence*)
MARIA Wonders will never cease!

SCENE 9

The Baron with the black armband appears, looking somewhat the worse for wear, tired and bitter. Maria notices him and stares at him in fascination.

SCENE 10

BARON (*gives her a very gallant greeting*) Salutations, my dear. I was a bit worried you might not turn up.
MARIA (*in an expressionless voice*) I gave my word of honor. (*silence*)
BARON (*recognizes Elizabeth*) Oh! (*raises his hat with a malicious grin*)
MARIA What? You already know my new girlfriend?
BARON "New?" (*to Elizabeth*) I believe we were trying to sell our corpse?
MARIA Corpse?
BARON (*smoothing out his rather crumpled black armband*) Yes, yes, we've all known better days. I had my business, sole agency for —
ELIZABETH (*grinning*) — corsets, perhaps?
BARON No, liqueurs. Now I'm kaput.
MARIA (*looking at herself in a pocket mirror by the light coming from the welfare agency's windows*) Hugo, haven't you noticed something about me?
BARON I'm afraid I couldn't quite say —
MARIA There! (*bares her teeth*) I've had two teeth crowned. There, at the front. They were all black and rotten — because the nerve was dead.
BARON (*with a suggestive smile*) You've changed for the better.
MARIA I'm happy with myself.

SCENE 11

A police detective appears, behind Maria, who is still looking at her crowns in her mirror. The Baron withdraws a little, and the detective waits for Maria to notice him; when she does she gives a slight start.

SCENE 12

DETECTIVE You're coming along with me. You know why.

MARIA (*without conviction*) I know nothing.
DETECTIVE Oh, so you know nothing then?
BARON And what about my cufflinks?
(*silence*)
MARIA (*softly*) Sweet Jesus.
BARON Who was it who stole them?
DETECTIVE Police. You're coming along with me.
MARIA (*glaring at the Baron*) You put the finger on me?
DETECTIVE Be quiet —
MARIA You? After I lent you three marks!? Three marks!
DETECTIVE Shut your mouth.
BARON (*with another gallant flourish*) Salutations, my dear. (*exit*)
MARIA You swine! You lousy swine!
DETECTIVE (*quickly puts the handcuffs on her*) Shut you face! Off we go! (*drags her off with him*)
MARIA Ouch!

SCENE 13

The policeman (Alfred Klostermeyer) comes running up to see what the screaming is about; he stops and sees Elizabeth; she sees him.

SCENE 14

POLICEMAN What was all that about?
ELIZABETH (*with a bitter smile*) Oh, nothing. A girl's just been arrested, that's all. For nothing.
POLICEMAN Come off it. Things like that don't happen.
ELIZABETH Nevertheless.
(*silence*)
ELIZABETH What are you staring at me like that for?
POLICEMAN (*with a smile*) Is that forbidden?
(*Silence*)
POLICEMAN Because you remind me — your manner, really — of someone I loved, someone who's gone to a better world —
ELIZABETH You've come over all mystical all of a sudden.

(*silence*)
POLICEMAN Which way are you going?
ELIZABETH Are you offering to see me home?
POLICEMAN I'm off duty now.
ELIZABETH I prefer to go alone.
POLICEMAN (*asks the question in all innocence*) Have you got something against the police?
ELIZABETH (*gives a slight start*) Why do you ask?
POLICEMAN Because you don't want me to see you home. Don't you see the police are necessary. There's a railway murderer hidden somewhere deep inside every one of us, you know.
ELIZABETH Not inside me.
POLICEMAN Oh, come off it.
ELIZABETH (*imitating him*) "Oh, come off it."
POLICEMAN (*with a smile*) You know, you're acting as if you'd been executed once already.
ELIZABETH No one cares about me.
POLICEMAN While there's life there's hope.
ELIZABETH That's just something people say.
(*silence*)
POLICEMAN And without faith, love, hope there's no life. It's logical. They're all bound up together.
ELIZABETH It's easy for you to talk, a policeman with a good steady job.
POLICEMAN We all have to die.
ELIZABETH And don't talk to me about love!
(*silence*)
POLICEMAN Just listen to me for a moment, will you? You see, I've been watching you here outside the welfare agency for several days now. Because you remind me of — of someone who was dear to me, someone who died.
ELIZABETH Who was this someone who died?
POLICEMAN My girlfriend.
(*silence*)
POLICEMAN We were like two turtledoves. But she had this liver thing and now I miss her, I really do miss her. Why are you smiling?

ELIZABETH Because.
(*silence*)
POLICEMAN You seem to be very bitter.
ELIZABETH I walk quickly.
POLICEMAN Walk quickly, then, I can walk quickly too.
(*A shot rings out in the distance, then another and another; someone screams. Silence.*)
POLICEMAN (*listening*) What was all that about? They must be shooting at each other again. This undeclared civil war is enough to drive you mad. I'll have to go and have a look, but I'll be back in no time. Wait for me.
ELIZABETH Okay.
POLICEMAN (*goes off to the right*)

SCENE 15

The Judge's Wife and His Honor the Judge come on from the left.
JUDGE'S WIFE Come on, Augustus, stop dragging behind. Now in you go and tell the welfare director that it's off for this evening because you have to spend some time with your better half for once.
JUDGE But I don't like going to the movies. Two whole hours without a cigar!
JUDGE'S WIFE But it's good for you! Just give a thought to your insides for once.
JUDGE I am thinking. The doctor warned me again only yesterday.
JUDGE'S WIFE And he warned me not to go up and down so many stairs, because of the trouble with my glands —
JUDGE (*interrupts her*) Do you have to go selling corsets?! Absolute nonsense!
JUDGE'S WIFE But I don't want to have to come begging to you for every penny.
JUDGE None of these modern ideas, if you please! And anyway, what do you know about begging? Now if you spent all day sentencing people who really are poor — often they're in trouble simply because they haven't got a roof over their heads —

JUDGE'S WIFE Then I wouldn't find them guilty.
JUDGE Hermione!
(*silence*)
JUDGE Okay, then. I'll go and tell the director our card game's off tonight because I have to spend some time with my better half. But you'll only have yourself to blame if it's all the usual sentimental rubbish, my little Minnie Mouse. (*goes into the welfare agency*)

SCENE 16

The Judge's wife notices Elizabeth. They stare at each other; Elizabeth does not want to know anyone from her past, but the Judge's Wife refuses to be put off.

SCENE 17

JUDGE'S WIFE That's funny, I think we've met —
ELIZABETH (*looks round anxiously*) Please — you don't know me —

JUDGE'S WIFE Don't worry. It's none of my business, but what did you get?
ELIZABETH Fourteen days.
JUDGE'S WIFE There. What did I tell you?
ELIZABETH Not suspended.
JUDGE'S WIFE Not suspended?
ELIZABETH Because I'd already been fined before. (*grins*) If only I knew what I'd done wrong —
JUDGE'S WIFE Oh, I know, I know. You don't have to tell me. One injustice after another — and you won't have another job, either?
ELIZABETH No. But just now I met a man, and he started telling me about his girlfriend who died — (*grins again*)
JUDGE'S WIFE That'd certainly be the best thing for you, marriage —

ELIZABETH (*in an expressionless voice*) I wouldn't say no.
JUDGE'S WIFE Congratulations are in order, then.
ELIZABETH We met by chance.

Faith, Love, Hope 217

JUDGE'S WIFE That's the way things start. Oh, I know all about that.
ELIZABETH Perhaps it's my big chance.
JUDGE'S WIFE And what does he do, this prospective fiancé?
ELIZABETH He's a state official.
JUDGE'S WIFE A state official? Does he know about your fourteen days in prison?
ELIZABETH No.
JUDGE'S WIFE You'll have to tell him, you know. Otherwise it might cause him difficulties in his career —
ELIZABETH Do you really think so?
JUDGE'S WIFE Definitely.
ELIZABETH There he comes.
JUDGE'S WIFE Where? — What? You mean a policeman? — Well, of course, it's no business of mine. All the best. (*withdraws some way away*)

SCENE 18

POLICEMAN (*returns; to Elizabeth*) Okay, I'm free now. They shot an innocent bystander. The times we live in! I often wonder —(*suddenly points to the Judge's Wife*) What does that woman want?
ELIZABETH (*lies*) I don't know her.
POLICEMAN But look at the way she's staring at us.
ELIZABETH Perhaps she's mixed us up with someone else. It's very easy to mix people up.
POLICEMAN That's true. Though if I were to mix people up — in my official capacity — it wouldn't do my career any good.
ELIZABETH Are they really that strict in the police?
POLICEMAN Really strict. So strict it's often even unfair. — Are you cold? Your teeth are chattering.
ELIZABETH Yes.
POLICEMAN Very?
ELIZABETH Pretty cold.
POLICEMAN I'd give you my jacket to wear, I don't need it, but it's not allowed.

ELIZABETH (*with a smile*) Your jacket's on duty all the time.
POLICEMAN When duty calls —
ELIZABETH Let's go. There's a chilly wind here. (*slowly off with the Policeman*)

SCENE 19

His Honor the Judge comes out of the Welfare agency
JUDGE'S WIFE (*suddenly gossipy*) Augustus, look! Over there! That's that girl I saw at Prantl's — you know, the fraud with the customs inspector and the insurance inspector?
JUDGE No idea.
JUDGE'S WIFE But you sentenced her —
JUDGE Could be.
(*silence*)
JUDGE'S WIFE But not giving her a suspended sentence, Augustus, that wasn't right —
JUDGE (*furious*) Right or wrong, you just mind your own business, Hermione!
(*dark*)

ACT FOUR

SCENE 1

Elizabeth's furnished room. The Policeman (Alfred Klostermeyer) is lying on the bed in his underpants, having a quiet snooze. Elizabeth is making coffee, glancing now and then at the white Michaelmas daisies in a vase beside the spirit stove. An October sun is shining outside, but the blinds are half drawn, creating the atmosphere of two loving hearts at peace with each other and the world.

SCENE 2

ELIZABETH (*sniffing the white Michaelmas daisies*) How they've lasted! Five days already! You know, I'd never have thought you'd buy Michaelmas daisies for me.
POLICEMAN I heard this voice inside me.
ELIZABETH Even so.
POLICEMAN You thought such a smart policeman would have to be a fickle gigolo? Only interested in a girl with lots of money? How wrong can you get! I respect a woman more when she depends on me, not the other way round. Do I get another kiss now?
ELIZABETH Yes.
POLICEMAN Is that coffee just about ready?
ELIZABETH Right away.
POLICEMAN (*takes the earphones from the bedside table and puts them on; hums the "Radetzky March" a military band is playing on the radio*) Just listen to that! I can see the boys marching!
ELIZABETH Alfred — there was a marvelous live broadcast yesterday — opera — Aida.
POLICEMAN (*puts the earphones back down on the bedside table*) So you didn't miss me at all?
ELIZABETH Oh, Alfred!
POLICEMAN Do I get another kiss?
ELIZABETH Here's your coffee. (*brings him a cup*) And here's your kiss. (*gives him a kiss and sits on the edge of the bed*)

POLICEMAN (*drinking his coffee with relish*) I'm just glad those stupid elections are over. On the alert all the time! Only the day before yesterday another of our men got shot.
ELIZABETH So many innocent people!
POLICEMAN It's the price we have to pay if we want law and order.
ELIZABETH I know injustice is inevitable because we human beings don't have true humanity — but there could be a bit less injustice.
POLICEMAN All this philosophy! What do you like best about me?
ELIZABETH Everything.
POLICEMAN Yes, but what word do you think suits me best?
ELIZABETH I don't know.
POLICEMAN Oh come on, you must know.
ELIZABETH You've changed a bit, Alfred. You used to be sadder before.
POLICEMAN In what way do you mean?
ELIZABETH Well, more melancholy.
POLICEMAN Oh, but I still am that! No problem there.
ELIZABETH Pardon me — (*gets up*)
POLICEMAN Where are you off to? Oh there. Feel free — burn your brassiere, unlace your corset!
ELIZABETH (*starts slightly*) Why d'you say corset?
POLICEMAN (*surprised*) Why not?
Silence.
ELIZABETH (*giving a smile*) I'm sorry, I'm jut a bit on edge today. (*goes off*)

SCENE 3

POLICEMAN (*alone*) Melancholy? More melancholy? What does she mean, even more melancholy?

SCENE 4

ELIZABETH (*returns*)
POLICEMAN That took a long time.
ELIZABETH A long time?

Faith, Love, Hope 221

POLICEMAN Nothing wrong, is there?
ELIZABETH What do you mean?
POLICEMAN I've always been careful, you know.
ELIZABETH Oh that.

SCENE 5

A knock at the door; the two loving hearts listen — there is another knock, firmer this time.
POLICEMAN Shh. There's no one at home.
ELIZABETH Who can it be?

SCENE 6

VOICE Open up, it's the police.
ELIZABETH Jesus and Mary!
POLICEMAN The police? And me here in my underpants! Just my luck! *quickly picks up his clothes and hides in the wardrobe.*

SCENE 7

The knocking on the door gets louder. Elizabeth opens and a man comes in. It is a police captain from the vice squad.

SCENE 8

POLICE CAPTAIN Knock and it shall be opened unto you. (*looks round and points to the unmade bed*) Did I wake you?
ELIZABETH Why?
POLICE CAPTAIN You know exactly why.
ELIZABETH I'm sorry, I'm not quite with it today.
POLICE CAPTAIN Some people are on night shift and have to catch up on their sleep during the day.
ELIZABETH What are you getting at?
POLICE CAPTAIN (*holding up a sock garter he found on the chair*) You wear garters, do you miss?
(*silence*)

ELIZABETH What do you want from me?
POLICE CAPTAIN On being released from prison you were required by the authorities to find *acceptable* means of supporting yourself within three weeks. But you haven't got a job, nor have you shown that you're looking for one.
ELIZABETH Why don't you go and pester people who have no means of supporting themselves!
POLICE CAPTAIN None of your soap-box oratory now! It's not against the law to have no visible means of support, but it is against the law if that represents a danger to the public order.
ELIZABETH But I'm not a danger to public order.
POLICE CAPTAIN That is open to question as long as we have no evidence as to your source of income.
ELIZABETH You don't need to worry. I'm being provided for.
POLICE CAPTAIN It is precisely the nature of this provision that we're interested in.
ELIZABETH But I've already told the authorities. My fiancé gives me twenty marks a week. That's what I live on.
POLICE CAPTAIN And who is this fiancé?
(*silence*))
POLICE CAPTAIN So you refuse to give his name?
ELIZABETH Yes.
POLICE MAN Might I ask why?
ELIZABETH Because I might possibly harm my fiancé's prospects.
POLICE CAPTAIN Oh, nice! Very nice! And what if I suggested these twenty marks might possibly be spread over several fiancés.
ELIZABETH That is an outrageous suggestion!
POLICE CAPTAIN Now just calm down, miss. You'll excuse me if I do a little indiscreet prying. (*suddenly opens the wardrobe; he is visibly unsurprised to find a man in it, but rather embarrassed when it turns out this man is a policeman in uniform jacket and cap, but with only his underpants on*)

SCENE 9

POLICEMAN (*stands to attention in the wardrobe*)
POLICE CAPTAIN You here?!

Faith, Love, Hope 223

POLICEMAN Everything the young lady said is true, captain.
(*silence*)
POLICE CAPTAIN (*to Elizabeth*) Would you mind leaving us alone for a few minutes.
ELIZABETH (*hesitates*)
POLICEMAN (*to Elizabeth*) Please.
ELIZABETH Okay. (*exit*)

SCENE 10

POLICE CAPTAIN So this is where you spend your idle hours?
POLICEMAN (*coming out of the wardrobe and hurriedly getting dressed.*) If I could perhaps just explain, captain — I'm sure there must be some mistake —
POLICE CAPTAIN Mistake? I think the mistake is your taking up with this woman. We've got our eye on her. We think she might belong to a certain class of ladies —
POLICEMAN Class of ladies?
POLICE CAPTAIN Probably.
(*silence*)
POLICEMAN (*with a smile*) No, captain, that's not —
POLICE CAPTAIN (*interrupting*) Do you know this young lady?
POLICEMAN Know her? Yessir!
POLICE CAPTAIN And intend to marry her?
POLICEMAN That is my intention, captain.
POLICE CAPTAIN How old are you?
POLICEMAN Twenty-four, sir.
POLICE CAPTAIN The old, old story.
POLICEMAN (*now fully dressed again*) But what she said about the twenty marks was the truth, sir.
POLICE CAPTAIN Eighty marks a month! And you don't exactly receive a princely salary.
POLICEMAN My parents help me out.
POLICE CAPTAIN What is your father?
POLICEMAN A cabinetmaker.
POLICE CAPTAIN Then I think you should have become a cabinetmaker.

POLICEMAN Why do you say that, sir?
(*silence*)
POLICE CAPTAIN I'm sorry to have to tell you this, but you seem to have no idea who that woman is you intend to get hitched to. Your young lady has already spent fourteen days in prison for fraud.
POLICEMAN In prison?
POLICE CAPTAIN For fraud. And she's had a fine. That a liaison with a policeman would seem desirable to a young lady like that is quite understandable. What it would do for your career, on the other hand —
POLICEMAN Yes, sir. I see, sir.
POLICE CAPTAIN There you are. (*opens the door and shouts*) You can come back in now.

SCENE 11

Elizabeth comes back in; she is already convinced it's all over. Silence.
POLICEMAN Fraud? Is that true?
ELIZABETH I know it's all over.
POLICEMAN Prison?
ELIZABETH Yes.
(*silence*)
POLICEMAN But why didn't you tell me, Elizabeth.
ELIZABETH What a goddam stupid question!
(*silence*)
POLICEMAN (*stands to attention*) My thanks, captain.
POLICE CAPTAIN Think nothing of it.
POLICEMAN (*clicks his heels and is about to leave*)
ELIZABETH Just a minute.
(*silence*)
POLICEMAN You lied to me and that's all that matters.
ELIZABETH No, it's your career, that's all that matters.
POLICEMAN No! But duty comes first and everything else is a long way behind. A long, long way behind.
(*silence*)

ELIZABETH But Alfred, before, when you were in the wardrobe, I was trying to protect you.
POLICEMAN Me?
ELIZABETH Us.
POLICEMAN Yourself. You were trying to protect yourself. At my expense. I know your kind.
(*silence*)
ELIZABETH (*grinning*) I just didn't want to lose you, Alfred dear —

POLICEMAN (*clicking his heels again*) Goodbye, captain. (*leaves quickly*)

SCENE 12

POLICE CAPTAIN That was really thoughtless of you, endangering the man's career like that —
ELIZABETH Thoughtless? And my career?
POLICE CAPTAIN You're surely not going to claim you're innocent?
ELIZABETH Oh no, I was cured of that illusion a long time ago. I'm sorry, but I just have to laugh. (*sits on the edge of the bed and laughs silently*)
POLICE CAPTAIN Have a good laugh. (*exit*)
(*dark*)

ACT FIVE

SCENE 1

The police station; after midnight.
The Policeman (Alfred Klostermeyer) is playing chess with his Buddy. It is raining outside and in the distance an orchestra is playing Chopin's popular Funeral March — until Scene 3.

SCENE 2

POLICEMAN (*listening*) Who's that playing?
BUDDY The radio.
POLICEMAN After midnight?
BUDDY Perhaps an American station. It's daytime there. Your move.
POLICEMAN Okay.
(*silence*)
POLICEMAN (*moves his rook*)
BUDDY (*thinks*) If I go there, he'll go here. If I go here, he'll go there. The sun was shining on the sea, shining with all his might. And that was odd because it was — G7 to c3. Check.
POLICEMAN You as well.
(*pause*)
POLICEMAN Who's move is it?
BUDDY Always the person's who asks.
(*pause*)
POLICEMAN (*standing up*) I resign.
BUDDY Resign? In that position?
POLICEMAN There's no way out.
BUDDY No way out?! D5 to d7! H2 to g4!
POLICEMAN Could be.

SCENE 3

BUDDY (*still looking at the chessboard*) You're giving up with that position? The man who always insists on playing every game out to the bitter end, even if it looks hopeless.
POLICEMAN I think I must be ill. I've been like this for some time. When I go to bed I wake up, and when I get up I fall asleep.
BUDDY Must be something to do with your nerves.
POLICEMAN (*with a wry smile*) I had a bit of trouble recently.
BUDDY At work?
POLICEMAN No. Personal. To do with a woman. You do everything for them, sacrifice everything to them — your hard-earned money, your free time, your most intimate feelings — and what is the result? You end up looking a fool.
BUDDY Nothing but ingratitude.
POLICEMAN Sometimes I wonder what's the point of it all.
BUDDY For God's sake, Alfred, that's the first step on the slippery slope.
POLICEMAN Why should I care. Look — I used to get on really well with my first girlfriend, and she went and died on me. That's the way thing are with me. One dies, the other lies. One disappointment after the other. I can't find anyone whose love's worthwhile.

SCENE 4

A third policeman comes in, bringing with him the Technician, who is completely drunk; the Laboratory Assistant is also there and also somewhat the worse for drink.
THIRD POLICEMAN Right then. Here we are.
LABORATORY ASSISTANT But my dear sergeant —
THIRD POLICEMAN (*interrupts him*) Quiet! (*to the other two policemen*) Disturbing the peace and insulting behavior toward a police officer.
LABORATORY ASSISTANT What do you mean, insulting behavior?
THIRD POLICEMAN Didn't he charge about, bellowing and hammering on the shutters with his stick and woke up the whole street? Didn't he call me a knuckleheaded asshole? Well, didn't he?

(*silence*)
LABORATORY ASSISTANT We're very sorry. This gentleman's sixty-two today, and all we wanted to do was to go out for a quiet celebration but, man proposes —
BUDDY (*with a grin*) and God disposes.
TECHNICIAN *bitter* And who's to blame? The senior technician, that's who!
THIRD POLICEMAN Silence! (*pointing to the chessboard*) Who won?
BUDDY Me.
THIRD POLICEMAN You? Against him? Not possible.
POLICEMAN My brain's on holiday today.
TECHNICIAN Gentlemen! Who's my enemy? The senior technician and the senior technician alone!
THIRD POLICEMAN That's enough. I don't want another peep out of you now.
BUDDY Why does he keep going on about this senior technician?
LABORATORY ASSISTANT That's the whole point. You see, I'm the assistant and the senior technician is this man here. He was promoted last month, but whenever he gets drunk, he forgets. The senior technician this senior technician keeps going on about came to a sticky end — he caught an infection, from a corpse, from Brno — the corpse that is —
THIRD POLICEMAN That's enough of that! Sit down while I take a statement.

SCENE 5

BOOKKEEPER (*comes rushing in*) Help, officer, help! There's a girl over there by the canal!
BUDDY By the canal?
THIRD POLICEMAN What girl?
BOOKKEEPER Suicide! We pulled her out of the water — that is, I didn't, someone else did. An intrepid young life-saver! I think she's still alive! There she is!

SCENE 6

Two men, one in a tuxedo, and the intrepid young life-saver appear carrying Elizabeth, whom they have pulled out of the canal. They lay her on a bench. The intrepid young life-saver is called Joe and is soaking wet and shivering with cold; one of the policemen gives him a blanket, which he wraps round himself. All of them, with the exception of the Technician, start fussing round Elizabeth. The policeman, Alfred Klostermeyer, goes over to her as well, recognizes her, and stares at her.

BOOKKEEPER I think she's still alive. Just!
THIRD POLICEMAN Quick! Artificial respiration!
LABORATORY ASSISTANT Let me help. I can do that. I did first-year medicine before the money ran out.
BUDDY Get on with it then!
TECHNICIAN And some brandy.
JOE For me too, please.
TECHNICIAN (*to Joe*) Takes some doing, diving into the water in the dark in the middle of November! A bold deed, sir. Intrepid, even.
JOE Oh, I was just doing what any normal human being would do. (*takes a swig from the brandy bottle*)
TECHNICIAN Too modest, too modest. (*takes the brandy bottle off him and turns to the Policeman*) Is that not right, general?
POLICEMAN I'm not a general.
TECHNICIAN Here's to our bold young life-saver! Prost. (*drinks*)
JOE (*to the Policeman*) I was just passing when I heard something go plop and I saw a silvery gleam in the water — her face. I jumped in right away and did the necessary. Any man would have done the same. You too.
POLICEMAN Of course.
TECHNICIAN It'll be in all the papers. Front page. Your picture. The intrepid life-saver! Here's to you! (*drinks again*)
THIRD POLICEMAN (*with Elizabeth*) Where's that brandy got to?
TECHNICIAN There you are.
JOE (*to the Policeman*) Could I make a call?

POLICEMAN Sure. There it is.
BUDDY (*comes over to the Policeman*) There's nothing on her apart from an out-of-date license for door-to-door sales.
TECHNICIAN A license? For door-to-door sales?

SCENE 7

The two men who helped carry Elizabeth in have already left; while all the others, apart from the Policeman and the Technician are occupied helping Elizabeth (artificial respiration etc.). Joe calls his mother.

JOE Hi, Mom! Is that you Mom? No, no, I know I got you out of bed, but it's nothing to get worried about — I've just saved the life of a girl who tried to commit suicide! What do you say to that? Intrepid, eh? It'll be in the paper, with my picture, just think of the publicity for the firm — free, too, and in all the papers. You still there? I'll be getting that motorbike now, won't I? What?! But you promised! We'll see?? Goodbye! (*hangs up, furious; aside*) Old cow!

SCENE 8

POLICEMAN Is she dead?
BUDDY I think she's still breathing.
LABORATORY ASSISTANT You'll see, you'll see.

SCENE 9

TECHNICIAN (*recognizes Elizabeth*) That's her. Sure as sure. The very one. (*turns to the Policeman, overcome with remorse*) You're the district attorney. I have —
POLICEMAN (*interrupting*) Just leave me in peace, will you!
TECHNICIAN But please, it won't take a moment — I've a confession to make. That young lady has been murdered.
POLICEMAN (*starts*) Murdered?
TECHNICIAN And I know who murdered her.
POLICEMAN What's all this nonsense?

(silence)
TECHNICIAN I was wrong you see, your Honor — about the customs inspector and the insurance inspector. An eye for an eye and a tooth for a tooth. Come on, do your duty and arrest me. Don't bother about a trial, just string me up!
LABORATORY ASSISTANT *(to the Policeman)* Now he's having one of his moral turns.
POLICEMAN *(to the Technician)* You swine!
TECHNICIAN Oh God! *(sits down in the corner)* The prisoner walked to the scaffold resigned to his fate. Do your duty, hangman! And pray for me, all you good people down there, so that you won't fall into temptation — and if you're about to do something stupid, just think of me — *(buries his head in his hands and stays like that, totally devastated)*

SCENE 10

THIRD POLICEMAN She's coming round!

SCENE 11

Elizabeth regains consciousness, but is still bemused; she sits up on the bench and looks round. At first she does not know what is going on and only gradually begins to remember.

SCENE 12

ELIZABETH *(to the Bookkeeper)* Who are you?
BOOKKEEPER Who? Me?
(silence)
THIRD POLICEMAN *(holding the brandy bottle out to her)* Here you are, miss —
ELIZABETH *(still staring at the Bookkeeper)* Who are you?
LABORATORY ASSISTANT *(to the Bookkeeper)* Come on, out with it!
BOOKKEEPER Me? I'm nothing?

ELIZABETH (*smiles*) Nothing — (*suddenly looking round anxiously*) Am I still alive?
BUDDY (*smiling*) You certainly are.
THIRD POLICEMAN (*still holding the brandy bottle out to her*) Here you are, miss —
ELIZABETH (*suddenly scrutinizes the Buddy with a look of horror*) What's that your wearing?
BUDDY (*somewhat bewildered*) What do you mean?
ELIZABETH Green, gray, and silver — Have I been arrested again? What have I done this time?
THIRD POLICEMAN Take it easy now. We're here to protect you. — Yes we are.
ELIZABETH (*in another world*) Who was that breathing on me?
BUDDY Wake up, miss — Hey, you only live once, why chuck yourself in the water?
ELIZABETH Did you —?
JOE I did.
(*silence*)
ELIZABETH Why can't you all just leave me alone?
JOE That's the thanks you get.
ELIZABETH I'd got away from it, and now it's starting all over again, and no one has responsibility for you, and your life's meaningless —
LABORATORY ASSISTANT (*touches her on the shoulder*) You mustn't give up hope. Everyone's life has a meaning, if not for themselves, then at least for others.
ELIZABETH Not mine.
LABORATORY ASSISTANT I'm sure it has.
ELIZABETH No.
LABORATORY ASSISTANT (*to the Buddy*) It really drives me mad when people contradict me like that. I'm dealing with dead people all day and you automatically start thinking about the meaning of life. As a laboratory assistant at the Anatomical Institute —
ELIZABETH (*interrupts him*) The Anatomical Institute? (*in a shrill voice*) And how is my old friend the technician? Still feeding the pigeons?

SCENE 13

TECHNICIAN Yes. (*gets up, very dignified though still swaying a little*) The pigeons sit on my shoulders and eat out of my hand, the canary sings and I've trained my snake. I have hutch full of white mice, and my three goldfish are called Anthony, Joseph, and Herbert. I must insist on the respect due to my position. People obviously don't know yet who I am. I am the senior technician, so remember that, if you please. And if I should happen to kill someone, then I'll deal with the matter myself. Alone with my God. I wish you all good morning. (*exit*)
ALL — (*apart from Elizabeth — automatically click their heels*) Goodbye, sir.

SCENE 14

ELIZABETH (*catches sight of her policeman, sits up and sinks her teeth into her own hand*)
LABORATORY ASSISTANT Hey, come on now!
BOOKKEEPER I think she must be going off her head.
JOE I mean, it's no laughing matter, the cold water at this time of year, in the pitch dark.
ELIZABETH (*slowly raises her hand to shade her eyes, as if she were being dazzled by the sun*) Is that you, Alfred?
(*silence*)
BUDDY What's up, Klostermeyer? Do you two know each other?
ELIZABETH Do we know each other?
(*silence*)
ELIZABETH Come on, tell them if you know me.
POLICEMAN We know each other.
ELIZABETH (*with a grin*) There's a good boy!
(*silence*)
ELIZABETH And how's the career coming along?
THIRD POLICEMAN (*to Alfred Klostermeyer*) What's all this about?
POLICEMAN Tell you later.
ELIZABETH Why later?
(*silence*)

POLICEMAN (*pulling on his white gloves*) I've got to go. The parade.
ELIZABETH Parade?
POLICEMAN Outside the Palace. It's almost light.
ELIZABETH It's still dark, Alfred.
POLICEMAN Everything's been cleared up between us.
ELIZABETH You think so?
POLICEMAN It's over.
(*silence*)
ELIZABETH The way you just left —
POLICEMAN No more now, please.
ELIZABETH (*with a bitter smile*) Why not?
(*silence*)
POLICEMAN Don't try to get at me by killing yourself. What's it to do with me if you threw yourself into the canal? I gave you a helping hand —
ELIZABETH (*interrupts him*) Chop your hand off, then.
(*silence*)
ELIZABETH I'm going now. Do you hear me, Alfred?
THIRD POLICEMAN (*blocks her way at the door*) Stop.
ELIZABETH (*stares at him*) Good night.
THIRD POLICEMAN No.
(*silence*)
ELIZABETH Let me go now.
THIRD POLICEMAN Where to?
ELIZABETH That's no concern of yours.
THIRD POLICEMAN In the state you're in? You're staying here. That's our duty.
ELIZABETH (*with another bitter smile*) Have I been arrested again?
BUDDY Not arrested. Taken into custody for your own protection, that's all.
ELIZABETH Protection?
THIRD POLICEMAN In your own best interest.
ELIZABETH Odd. There you all are fussing around and you can't even get me a license to sell corsets legitimately — (*grins*)
LABORATORY ASSISTANT Now you're being childish.

ELIZABETH I don't mean it personally, for the moment I'm beyond that — (*suddenly shouting at Alfred*) Don't stare at me like that! Get out of my sight, otherwise I'll put out my own eyes! Don't think I threw myself in the canal because of you, you and your great career! I threw myself in the canal because I had nothing left to eat. If I'd had enough to eat, do you think I'd have even spat in your direction?! Don't look at me like that!! (*throws the brandy bottle at his eyes, but misses*) There!
BUDDY (*grasping her arm*) Hey, stop that!
ELIZABETH Let go of me!
JOE No you don't!
ELIZABETH (*screaming*) Let go! Let go!
THIRD POLICEMAN Silence!
JOE Ouch! She bites!
LABORATORY ASSISTANT What? Biting are you? Biting!
ELIZABETH (*draws back, cowed*)
BOOKKEEPER She's bitten the man who saved her life.
ELIZABETH (*bares her teeth*)

SCENE 15

In the distance is the sound of marching to a band, which is playing the march "Old Comrades." The music dies away; Elizabeth is sitting in a chair, bowed down.

SCENE 16

POLICEMAN The parade — (*puts his helmet on*) We'll have to get our skates on.
BUDDY There's still time, Klostermeyer. Wait for us — (*puts his white gloves on*)
THIRD POLICEMAN We have to go too.
LABORATORY ASSISTANT What's that rumbling noise?
BOOKKEEPER The girl's stomach.
THIRD POLICEMAN (*to the Buddy*) You got something here?
BUDDY Yes. (*takes a sandwich out of his jacket pocket and gives it to Elizabeth*)

ELIZABETH (*takes it and nibbles at it apathetically*)
THIRD POLICEMAN (*putting on his white gloves*) That good?
ELIZABETH (*gives him an apathetic smile; suddenly she drops the sandwich and collapses onto the table*)
LABORATORY ASSISTANT Whoops!
THIRD POLICEMAN Hey! (*he and the Laboratory Assistant are trying to help Elizabeth*)
BUDDY It's just a dizzy fit.
BOOKKEEPER Probably the stomach —
LABORATORY ASSISTANT A weak heart —
BOOKKEEPER Heart or stomach, it all comes down to the same thing in the end.
JOE It's no laughing matter, diving into the ice-cold water, in November, in the pitch dark —
LABORATORY ASSISTANT (*to Elizabeth*) Come on, don't die on us —

ELIZABETH (*comes to again; a weak smile*) I'd like to speak to someone in charge.
THIRD POLICEMAN Someone in charge?
ELIZABETH (*nods*) It's urgent. People say things are going to get worse, but I'm not going to let that get me down. (*waves her hands about as if she were trying to shoo away some flies*) What're all these black worms doing flying around? (*dies peacefully*)

SCENE 17

BOOKKEEPER (*goes up to the dead Elizabeth on tiptoe and knocks on the table-top; gently*) Come in, miss, come in.
THIRD POLICEMAN I fear the worst.
POLICEMAN (*takes off his helmet*)
LABORATORY ASSISTANT (*bending over Elizabeth*) She's gone. Probably the heart. We'll see at work tomorrow, of course.
JOE A waste of time and effort — (*exit*)

SCENE 18

POLICEMAN   A waste — (*goes over to the dead body of his Elizabeth and strokes her hair*) Poor kid. I have all the bad luck. I have all the bad luck.
BOOKKEEPER
I'm going I know not where,
I'll die I know not when.
I'll live I know not how long,
How come I'm singing a cheerful song? (*exit*)

SCENE 19

LABORATORY ASSISTANT   A poet.
THIRD POLICEMAN   It's still raining.
BUDDY   It's going to be a wet parade.
POLICEMAN   Probably.
LABORATORY ASSISTANT   Well, I'll say goodbye now. (*exit*)

SCENE 20

The sound of marching again, outside the station this time, still to the march "Old Comrades." The three policemen put on their helmets and leave the station — as we know, they have to go to the parade. Only Alfred Klostermeyer casts one last glance back at his dead girlfriend. Curtain.

Afterword

With Hungarian and Croatian, German and Czech ancestry, Ödön von Horváth (1901-1938) was, as he called himself, "a typical Austro-Hungarian mixture." This multinational background was also echoed in his upbringing: his father was a Hungarian diplomat and his early years were marked by frequent moves, from Fiume (now Rijeka in Croatia) to Belgrade and Budapest, then to Munich, Bratislava, Budapest again and Vienna.

He went to Munich University in 1919 and began writing soon after. In 1924 he moved to Berlin, which in the 1920s was the center of lively, not to say frenetic cultural activity, especially in the theater. His first play was performed in 1926 (*Das Buch der Tänze* — The Book of Dances) and by the end of the decade he had established himself on the German stage. It was in the early 1930s that the four plays contained in this volume appeared. They are his most important plays and the ones on which his reputation is founded.

After Hitler came to power in 1933 Horváth left Germany, but returned in 1934 and compromised with the regime there in order to work in Germany. He even, briefly, was a member of the official writers' organization of the Third Reich, but none of his plays were performed and he worked under a pseudonym in films. It was made clear to him that the Nazis regarded him as *persona non grata*.

In 1935 he moved to Vienna and, after Hitler's troops occupied the country in 1938, set off on an odyssey through Europe which eventually took him to Paris. He was killed during a thunderstorm by a falling branch from a tree on the Champs Élysées in June of that year.

After the war Horváth was largely a forgotten figure until his works were rediscovered in the early 1960s, leading to his recognition, along with Brecht, as one of the most important writers for the German theater in the 1930s.

Horváth remained a Hungarian citizen throughout his life, but all his literary works were written in German, the southern German of Austria and Bavaria. He described German as his "mother tongue," presumably having actually learned it from his mother, who had part-German background, although he said he could not write it until the age of fourteen when he went to school in Munich.

Most of Horváth's early plays were overtly political in theme and left-wing in sympathy. For example, he dramatized a tragedy in which workers were killed during the construction of a cable car (*Die Bergbahn* — The Cable Car); in another he portrayed a member of one of the right-wing paramilitary organizations (*Sladek der schwarze Reichswehrmann* — Sladek, Soldier in the Black Army).

His later plays however, although still betraying sympathy with the situation of the exploited classes, are more concerned with the way language is used for self-deception. The clichés and hollow phrases the characters — especially the male characters — employ reveal to the audience, though never to the characters themselves, the crude self-interest, cowardice or plain emptiness beneath.

To his four best-known plays which use this technique (the four plays contained in this collection) he gave the designation *Volksstück*, "popular play," that is, a play for and about ordinary people. There was a tradition of this kind of play in Austria going back into the first half of the nineteenth century, when they often had a satirical edge, especially in the work of Johann Nestroy (1802-1862). By the early twentieth century, however, they had tended more and more to become vehicles for a conservative, anti-modern outlook. Horváth maintained he was not going back to tradition but creating his own, new genre of "popular play."

In *The Italian Evening* (*Italienische Nacht*, first performed 1931) it is the complacency of the old guard of the Socialist Party, comfortably installed in their municipal offices and Party positions, that is the target. They are organizing a convivial evening with Italian food and wine in the garden of the inn where they regularly hold meetings, while the right-wing nationalist organization is holding military exercises. When the fascists threaten to disrupt the party, the men show their cowardice; the only person to stand up to the fascists is the city councilman's put-upon wife. At the last minute, the younger Socialists, who have been thrown out by the senior Party members, save the situation, at which the Socialist leaders slump back into their old complacency.

Horváth's best-known play, Tales from the Vienna Woods (*Geschichten aus dem Wiener Wald*, first performed in 1931), demolishes the myth of the *gemütlich* Viennese with their hearts of gold. This self-image finds expression in the Strauss waltzes, the schmaltzy popular songs and folk songs which are to be heard throughout the piece. Horváth strips away this sentimentality to reveal the lack of true sentiment beneath. Selfishness, lust not love and a latent brutality prove to be the true motivation behind the characters' actions.

Casimir and Caroline (*Kasimir und Karoline*, first performed in 1932) shows the reality behind another myth, that of the supposedly democratic nature of the Munich *Oktoberfest*. One businessman indulges in false sentimentality, saying "You get a porter sitting next to a counsellor, a businessman next to a tradesman, a minister next to a laborer — that's what I call democracy," while tucking into the roast chicken, schnapps and beer the poorer workers, not to mention the unemployed, cannot afford.

The other focus of *Casimir and Caroline* is the relations between the sexes. The motto of the play is a quotation from Saint Paul's First Epistle to the Corinthians, "And love never ends" ("charity never faileth" in the King James version). In this vision "love never ends" not because of the depth of true feeling, but because it is a kind of merry-go-round, a Schnitzlerian sexual "round dance" from partner to partner. Despite the clarity of his dissection of human emotion, however, Horváth still manages to create sympathy for his characters, who are more weak prisoners of society and its language than amoral libertines.

Horváth's final *Volksstück*, *Faith, Love, Hope* (*Glaube, Liebe, Hoffnung*, original premiere in 1933 canceled; first performed 1936) has a reference to the same chapter of Corinthians in the title ("faith, hope and charity" in the older King James version). He reverses the order of the three qualities, suggesting that the greatest of the three is hope, though it seems doomed to eternal disappointment.

The play is based on a real incident Horváth came across and once again shows woman as the victim. Elizabeth is trapped in a vicious circle. She is a traveling saleswomen in corsetry, but she cannot afford the money for a license. She is caught and fined, and so needs more money to pay the fine, as well as for a license. All she has to sell is her body. Whereas Marianne, in *Tales from the Vienna Woods*, does this in time-honored fashion by appearing in a strip show, Elizabeth tries, without success, to get an advance on her dead body from the Anatomical Institute.

The people around her are not entirely uncaring, but nobody has love or charity strong enough to help her to break out of the situation in which society has entrapped her. She throws herself in the river and dies — the Anatomical Institute gets her body free. A bleak little poem quoted by one of the characters could stand as a motto for the rather pessimistic picture of humanity all Horváth's *Volksstücke* present:

I'm going I know not where,
I'll die I know not when.
I'll live I know not how long,
How come I'm singing a cheerful song?

Despite their localized settings and language, Horváth's plays thus have a timeless relevance in the way they show how human hopes are thwarted by the combination of social constrictions and personal weakness. But they are also anchored in the situation and events of the time (fascists and socialists in *The Italian Evening*, German nationalist undertones in *Tales from the Vienna Woods*, unemployment in *Casimir and Caroline* and *Faith, Love, Hope*). Seen as products of the situation in central Europe in the 1930s, what they show is not so much the specific political details of the rise of fascism as the potential receptiveness to fascism of these shallow, self-deceiving individuals.

This could well be one reason for his neglect in the postwar years, especially among the Austrians, who wanted to see themselves as the victims rather than the perpetrators or willing beneficiaries of Nazism. A performance of *Tales from the Vienna Woods* in Vienna just after the war led to a riot among the audience. Horváth's stripping away of the comfortable self-image enshrined in language and popular culture had the ability to strike a still very raw nerve.

Michael Mitchell

Ariadne Press
Drama Series

Three Late Plays
By Arthur Schnitzler
Translated by G.J. Weinberger
ISBN 0-929497-52-X

Plays and Poems
By Oskar Kokoschka
Translated by Michael Mitchell
ISBN 1-57241-041-8

*Professor Bernhardi
and Other Plays*
By Arthur Schnitzler
Translated by G.J. Weinberger
ISBN 0929497-70-8

Five Plays
By Gerald Szyszkowitz
Translated by Todd C. Hanlin, Heidi Hutchinson, Joseph McVeigh
ISBN 0-929497-69-4

*Paracelsus
and Other One-Act Plays*
By Arthur Schnitzler
Translated by G.J. Weinberger
ISBN 0-929497-96-1

Prince and Plays
By Henry Gregor
(Prince Starhemberg)
Translated by Harvey I. Dunkle
ISBN 1-57241-033-7

The Final Plays
By Arthur Schnitzler
Translated by G.J. Weinberger
ISBN 1-57241-029-9

*The Holy Experiment
and Other Plays*
By Fritz Hochwälder
ISBN 1-57241-053-1

*Anthology of Contemporary
Austrian Folk Plays*
Includes: Veza Canetti, Peter Preses/Ulrich Becher, Peter Turrini, Felix Mitterer, Gerald Szyszkowitz
ISBN 0-929497-67-8

*New Anthology of Contemporary
Austrian Folk Plays*
Includes: Heinz R. Unger, Thomas Baum, Friedrich C. Zauner, Elfriede Jelinek, Peter Rosei
ISBN 1-57241-029-5

Ariadne Press
Drama Series
(continued)

Three Radio Plays
By Ingeborg Bachmann
Translated by Lilian Friedberg
ISBN 1-57241-079-5

An Anthology of Plays
By Werner Schwab
Translated by Michael Mitchell
ISBN 1-57241-064-7

*Siberia
and Other Plays*
By Felix Mitterer
ISBN 0929497-68-6

Alpine Glow
By Peter Turrini
Translated by Richard Dixon
ISBN 0-929497-95-3

*The Wild Woman
and Other Plays*
By Felix Mitterer
Translated by Todd C. Hanlin
and Heidi Hutchinson
ISBN 1-5724002-7

*Shooting Rats,
Other Plays
and Poems*
By Peter Turrini
Translated by Richard Dixon
ISBN 0-929497-98-8

"It's Up to Us"
Collected Works of Jura Soyfer
Edited by Horst Jarka
Includes his plays
ISBN 0-929497-55-4

*The Slackers
and Other Plays*
By Peter Turrini
Translated by Richard Dixon
ISBN 0-929497-48-1

Visit our Website:

http://ariadnepress.com

Dirt
By Robert Schneider
Translated by Paul F. Dvorak
ISBN 1-57241-023-X

Made in the USA
San Bernardino, CA
31 October 2016